MY CLASS AND OTHER ANIMALS

BY

KELVIN REYNOLDS

BURWELL XMAS BOOK FLOOD

COPYRIGHT 2023

ALL RIGHTS RESERVED

DEDICATED TO THE MEMORY OF

HELGA ROBERTS

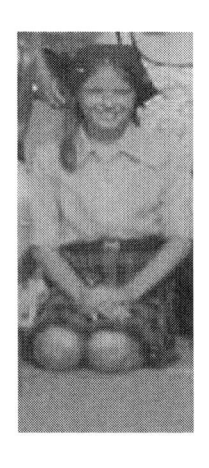

1963-1986

WHO WAS WITH ME FROM THE FIRST DAY

Introduction

Sawston Village College was officially opened by HRH Edward, Prince of Wales, in October 1930. He believed that he was to open a brand new Cambridge University college and he is seen here walking down the drive, pictured on the right carrying his hat, unsmiling and very unimpressed. He allegedly told an official 'this is a bloody kindergarten!'

It is a very unique college, embracing the whole community. It was originally designed to be a beautiful building, with no gates or barriers, set in a rural location in 1930 with lessons and activities during the day and in the evening. In this book I will focus on my time teaching at the college from 1975 onwards.

The school still thrives today as a Comprehensive coeducational for 11-16 years and I had no idea in 1975 what teaching here would mean for me or that I would still be there forty years later!

I cover a wide range of topics and compare Sawston with the narrow and rigid education I received at a grammar school in Cambridge. The emphasis on animals also reflects the location of the school set in a rural community. Many chapters will feature an animal.

    The main emphasis will always be on humour, the fun we had, the animals we met, and the wonderful students who touched my life.

I feel very privileged to write and share this story. Thank you Sawston VC.

Chapter One

Charlotte and the Sheep

A crisp February morning. Period 1, Year 8 History. The mobile classroom is freezing today, although I use the term 'classroom' very loosely. It is, in fact, a metal box with one door and two windows that don't open or close properly. It is pressure cooker hot in summer and icebox cold in winter. It has a heater, a metal thing powered by calor gas with a guard that sits in the corner. To get the contraption working you have to press button A which strikes a pilot light and then the burners ignite. That's the theory. There's a sticky label on the side that says if it doesn't fire up first time try a second time and it will ignite. Actually it should say if it doesn't light first time try striking the button 187 times and it might just work. Usually it doesn't. And in the days before mobile phones there's no way of letting anyone know, so I have to trek to the main office and alert the caretaker who may or may not appear before the end of the lesson. By which time, the pupils have long lost any interest they may have had in the causes of the English Civil war!

On this particular day I let the children wear their outdoor coats which for some reason they regard as a special treat. And despite the cold, they have all opened their books and copied the title from the roller blackboard. All except Charlotte. She looks really distracted and agitated and keeps looking out of the window. Normally she is a very good pupil, well behaved who produces beautiful work in her notebook. The only advantage of residing in this metal container for all my lessons is that it is detached and overlooks a farmer's field full of sheep. I ask Charlotte if she is OK. 'I need to go!' she says standing up.

'Look Charlotte if you need to go to the toilet that's fine-'

'No, you don't understand. I need to go over there.' She points to the field. 'There's a sheep over there upside down and she's dying!'

'What?'

By now Charlotte's heading for the door. 'That sheep is on its back and

she can't get up, she will die if I don't help her.'

I follow her out of the door, 'Charlotte, please come back, we can't do anything. I'll let the farmer know at break time-' Too late. Charlotte has pushed her way through a hedge and is now sprinting across the field. And worse still, ten seconds later, twenty three other excited pupils are following her.

'Come on Sir, we've got to help her, it's her dad's farm!' shouts Ben.

And so we end up in the middle of this field, surrounded by a group of curious sheep, munching grass. Right in the centre is young Charlotte. I'm worried that she might get hurt. She is the smallest girl in the class. I know nothing about sheep and worry that the rest of the flock may become aggressive towards us. Charlotte ignores my warnings, grabs the sheep's legs and body and in one movement rolls it back on its side. We all look on in amazement as she helps the animal get back on its feet. The sheep walks off to join the rest of the flock, none the worse for her fall and Charlotte is surrounded by cheering students.

'Wow! That was amazing,' I tell her as we make our way back to the classroom., 'How did you know what to do?'

Her little face lights up, 'Done it before. Sometimes if they are pregnant, they slip or roll over and then they can't stand up. If they can't breathe properly they will die.'

I learnt something really special that day about sheep, about Charlotte, and about the many hidden skills and talents that children possess. From then on, every lesson I had with that group we always peered out of the window first to make sure the sheep were all OK!

Every child has a special gift, everyone. And whatever that gift is, we as teachers, must find ways to promote and help them develop those special talents. It could change someone's life.

Chapter Two

The First Day

1R   Day One.....2nd September 1975.

In front of me, 32 anxious faces and nervous smiles, not knowing what to expect. 33 if you count me as well! IR, their first experience of secondary school. And after four years training it was a wonderful moment when I closed the door knowing this was my first class. I was now a fully qualified teacher and I was getting paid for it. They certainly looked the part in their sparkling new uniforms. The uniform was either blue or grey. Ties were compulsory for boys, girls rarely wore ties. What was interesting is that no girl wore trousers in any year group in the early seventies. This was something that would come much later.

The previous day I had put up a few Salvador Dali posters on the walls, that I bought from Athena. The classroom had brand new desks and tables, each seating two pupils and at the back of the room was a row of metal lockers that gave the classroom an American high school feel. After taking the register and hoping I had pronounced the names correctly, the next job was the timetable. Today, students receive their timetables all printed out in July with group settings listed in all subjects, ready for a smooth start to the term in September. Not so in 1975.

Behind my desk was a blackboard fixed to the wall. It had been painted over the summer holidays but within weeks the shiny black paint would became a chalky grey covered in dust and marks. The timetable had to be written on the blackboard for the pupils to copy into their notebooks which meant drawing lines across the board to create forty blocks to insert the lessons. Eight lessons a day, each lasting 35 minutes, quite short with a few double periods. My hand writing is terrible and struggling with this timetable was a nightmare. I was supposed to have a large blackboard ruler to draw lines with but it didn't materialise so I had to draw them myself. They were all over the place and then I had to fill in the subject blocks in very narrow spaces. GEOG, HIST, MATH and so on. I'm sure it looked a right mess, not a good introduction to my form. But they were pleasant and patient, especially as copying the timetable took up most of the morning.

There were four lessons in the morning with a fifteen minute break and four in the afternoon, with an hour for lunch. There was also an afternoon registration. Eight lessons a day might sound a lot compared to the five one hour lessons a day which is the current situation at the college. But the actual time spent in the classroom in 1975 was 280 minutes a day compared with 300 minutes today, which means that our current students are studying one hour twenty minutes longer each week compared with 1975.

Lunchtimes were very different in the seventies. The procedure was as follows: students queued to get their meal from serving hatches, and were then guided to a table. The wooden tables were pushed together to seat eight people, each table had to be filled up before you could start your meal. Pupils couldn't pick and choose where to sit, which was sometimes annoying if your friend was placed on another table. The meals were generally very good, quite wholesome and excellent value for five shillings a weeks, something that all form tutors had to collect every Monday morning. Teachers were offered a free meal providing they sat with the pupils, that wasn't a problem. I found it quite enjoyable, another way of getting to know my form. No pizzas available then, mainly potatoes, greens and meat. On Fridays it was usually fish and chips. I can't recall many pupils bringing a packed lunch.

So what didn't we have in 1975? No televisions in the classroom, no whiteboards, no overhead projectors. And of course, no computers. No pocket calculators, in fact the only calculator was a large machine kept in the lower school office, a mechanical thing that looked like a shop till. And as far as the kids were concerned, no internet, no mobiles (except mobile classrooms!) no daytime television, no facebook, no WhatsApp, no Instagram! No Love Island! The class of 1975 didn't miss all these things because we never had them!

The children in my first form are now nearly sixty years old!
But fifty years ago, most children felt very nervous about starting secondary school. They worried about new subjects and homework, being placed in a class without their friends, getting used to several teachers instead of one. And in many respects things are still the same for young students starting secondary school today.

And so my first day of teaching came to an end. I drove home to Cambridge, tired but very happy and still on a high. I really liked my form and loved the atmosphere in the school. I had no idea I would still be there teaching forty years later!

1R   MY FIRST FORM

It seemed only right to feature them on the front cover as these young people were my first class, the first thirty two children out of an estimated ten thousand that would pass through my classroom door in the years that followed.

I can't remember everybody's names but I'll do my best
BACK ROW: Daphne Clark, Deborah Peirce, Tracy Goddard, Dawn Hughes, Olufemi, Peter Ashcroft, Stephen Capes, Stephen Summerlin, John Moult, Geoffrey Maskell
MIDDLE ROW: Jennifer Willis, Ruth Owen, Deborah Elmer
FRONT ROW: Karen Kinsey, Sandra Gent, Tanya Gale, Helga Roberts.
Astrid. And one or two I can't distinguish obscured at the back.

Chapter Three

Biscuit meets the Chief Inspector and it doesn't end well....

In the days before health and safety regulations many classrooms in the eighties had their own pets, especially primary schools. We also had our fair share at Sawston, a guinea pig and rabbit run outside, plus gerbils and hamsters in the biology labs which the pupils used to look after every day. And one person would volunteer to look after the animals during the holidays. By this time I had been upgraded from my temporary tin box to a purpose built history block, comprising four class rooms and a staff room. But it was far from perfect. The windows were very small, built to conserve energy which seemed like a good idea at the time. Even ahead of its time. Unfortunately, the classrooms were so dark we had to keep the lights on in the block all day. The metal framed windows were in two parts, a simple slide up and down mechanism to open them. A serious flaw meant that sometimes the top window didn't latch properly and the frame would come crashing down, on one occasion narrowly missing a girl's fingers. Also, the block itself only had one central door at the front of the building which meant that during lesson change overs every 50 minutes, about 120 pupils would be trying to squeeze through the door to get out of the block while another 120 would be trying to push their way in. Total chaos until we established a traffic light system of entry and exit.

But it was in this block, having left my freezing mobile behind, where I got my first classroom pet, a gerbil named Biscuit. He was surplus to requirements from the biology department who had already got four. The department head told me that Biscuit had to be separated from the other gerbils because they didn't like him. We spruced up his cage, got him a wheel and installed a little red and yellow plastic house where he spent most of the day asleep. I used to get him out at least once a day and carry him around the classroom in my jacket pocket while I was teaching a lesson. Then he would pop his head out of the top of the pocket or sometimes he would go up my sleeve. I often took him outside when I was on playground duty but I always had to be careful if he curled up and went to sleep in my pocket in case someone should accidentally barge into me. Fortunately that never happened.

However, over a period of months Biscuit's constant gnawing created holes in my pocket and shredded the cuffs of my jacket. The kids loved Biscuit and all was well until the day the Inspector came, not any inspector but the Chief County Inspector himself. This was in the days before Ofsted, and occasionally the hierarchy from Shire Hall would visit each school to check on progress and offer advice in each subject area.

I found out the day before that Mr Duggan would be spending the day with the history department, visiting each class. It was at break time the day before the inspector's visits when Roy, our Head of Department, handed out the timetable for Mr Duggan's visit. I can still see the single typed sheet to this day. Under my name, period 5 last lesson of the day, 9N4 History.

I was like..'Nooo..not them, not period 5. They won't do any work, we'll get a terrible report.(meaning I would get a terrible report!), Please Roy, can I swap classes with you and have 8S1 just for tomorrow?' The answer of course, was 'No'. The Inspector had already decided on which lessons and which teachers he wanted to see.

So I decided on a strategy when I taught the class that afternoon, twenty four hours before the dreaded visit. The current topic I was teaching was the Agricultural Revolution in the 18th century.

After settling them down, which always took about

ten minutes, lowering my voice and looking very serious I started to explain what would happen.

'Tomorrow, the Chief Inspector is coming in to see you. He is the Chief Inspector of the whole county, very important man. He will be making a report on your progress and behaviour in history which will be sent to the Head and also to your parents. (All lies of course) I cannot emphasise enough how important this is. So it's vital that you revise your notes on farming pioneers for homework tonight and make sure your exercise books are fully up to date by tomorrow.'

Unusually the class received this information in silence until Nick, sitting in his usual place at the front, piped up,

'Is this inspector bloke coming to see you, 'cos you're the teacher?'

'Oh no, this isn't about me at all,' I said, shaking my head, 'this is all about you.' The others started mumbling amongst themselves but then Nick thumped the desk. 'Oi! Shut up everyone and listen. This inspector bloke is coming in tomorrow and if we don't do our work and start messing around Mr Reynolds will get the sack.'

'No, I won't get the sack, it's not about me...'

'So everyone's like gotta be good tomorrow and then Mr Reynolds won't get the sack.' The others all nodded and agreed, I stood there with an embarrassed smile on my face realising that they had sussed me out in about five minutes. I would like to think that the class were acting out of altruistic motives although it was probably the fact that I didn't give them a hard time, and no homework, it was a case of the devil you know.

And so the day dawned. The Chief Inspector duly arrived, briefly introduced himself and then went into a meeting with our Principal and Head of department before commencing his lesson observations. He was wearing a dark blue suit, a maroon tie and polished black shoes you could see your face in. He didn't smile or attempt to put us at ease in any way. I tried to focus on my other lessons as the clock ticked on. I read my notes over and over again. I tidied up the shelves at the back and placed a vacant chair ready for his highness when he arrived. I made pristine copies of an 18th century village map for every pupil in the class, plus diagrams of various agricultural implements,but I knew that farming pioneers would hardly likely stimulate their interest. Hence the constant whine every lesson. 'When are we going to do the war? or something interesting.'

By lunchtime Mr Duggan had observed all my colleagues, his written report would not be completed for another couple of weeks but each history teacher was given a feedback at the end of the lesson. By all accounts the inspection so far had gone very well for everyone. Just me to go.

I didn't eat most of my lunch, just drank some water and got to my classroom early, I gave out all the textbooks and photocopies for every pupil. Then sat and waited for Armageddon as the minutes ticked by.

They shuffled in as the bell sounded, mostly together which was unusual, eyes searching around for the Inspector who hadn't yet arrived.

'Where's the Inspector bloke?' asked Nick, arriving last, I was half hoping he might be away today.

'He'll be along soon, now let's all settle down and focus on the task in hand, should we?' And for once they did just that. The first task was to complete the village map and annotate the farming changes and stick the diagrams in their books. Ten minutes into the lesson a brief knock and the door opened. Mr Duggan strode across the classroom and found the vacant chair at the back of the room. He carried a clipboard and made a few notes then took a walk around the room, occasionally stopping and talking to some of the pupils. He sat down again as it was time for the oral part of the lesson, the part I was dreading most, the question and answer session.

'Why did Jethro Tull invent the seed drill?' Up went a dozen hands.

'Susie?'

'So he could plant seeds in straight lines and they would grow properly and the birds couldn't get them.'

'Excellent. Well done, Suzie. What about our second pioneer, Turnip Townshend, what did he do?'

Again a forest of hands shot up. 'Lee?'

'Because you can't grow wheat in the field every year because it gets exhausted so he planted turnips which is a root crop, then people could eat the turnips or put them in soup and the field wasn't wasted.'

'Brilliant, well done.' I smiled and briefly glanced at the Inspector. This was going really well. And then Nick put his hand up.

'What about that Bakewell bloke?' he asked. The previous week he had made countless jokes about Bakewell tarts and not the jammy biscuit version either.

'Yes, I was moving on to him next, he's also very important because he..' I said, trying to stop Nick saying any more.

'Because,' said Nick interrupting and looking down at his notes, 'because he bred that Leicester sheep which was huge and had good meat for the market, and all good strong sheep were kept together on his farm and he made a profit from..from..se ..selective breeding.'

'Excellent, Nick, I see your homework notes are up to date. Well done.'

Nick leaned back in his chair, his face beaming. It was all going very well, and the class moved on to the final task, which was to present a newspaper account of the farming pioneers of the 18th century with interviews with fictional villagers. Apart from a few murmurs, the class worked in silence, an amazing feat for 9N4. Mr Duggan added to his notes on the clipboard. I glanced at my watch, only ten minutes remaining, Probably my best lesson ever ever with 9N4. And that's when Biscuit woke up.

His whiskery cheeks emerged from his plastic house. It was though he was determined not to be left out of the inspection. He sucked at his water bottle. Then he started scratching at the bottom of his cage before jumping into his wheel. Biscuit loved his wheel but today he decided he would break all records for speed. The cage started to vibrate as Biscuit propelled himself around the wheel, his little legs working furiously. At first Mr Duggan turned round and glanced at the cage before continuing his notes. But worse was to come. Biscuit was kicking up a layer of dust from his cage that spread into the air. Mr Duggan started to sneeze. And sneeze and sneeze. At first the students showed only a mild interest. But the layer of dust thickened and the sneezes got louder, every three seconds a deep, rasping roar. The giggles soon spread to every row.

I'm on the front line, not actually knowing what to do next. I made my way to the back and asked the usual stupid question 'Are you all right?' when plainly he was not all right, he was standing up now, his crimson face covered by his handkerchief. Biscuit meanwhile carried on with his mission to exterminate the Chief Inspector. I knew I had to get Mr Duggan out of the classroom as soon as possible, I picked up his clip board, apologising profusely, and ushered him to the door, his eyes streaming, the lesson now completely lost.

He was still sneezing violently when we arrived at reception. The school nurse was called (yes we still had the funds for a school nurse in the eighties) and she recommended emergency treatment immediately, poor Mr Duggan was soon on his way to A and E, where I understand he was given injections and medication to control the symptoms of what had been a severe allergic reaction.

The good news was that Mr Duggan was discharged after a couple of hours and sent home. I went home thinking, that was the worst day ever. Would I still have a career tomorrow?

Most of the staff were sympathetic and saw the funny side of the situation, but I was dreading the written report that was to arrive a week later. Mr Duggan did actually state that my lesson overall was well planned and the students were 'motivated and well behaved.' I framed that bit. However, he was very unhappy about me keeping a small rodent in the classroom and pointed out that it could have been a child who had suffered a bad reaction.

It was the end of classroom life for Biscuit who was taken home by Samantha in my form, where he lived for another few months. I missed seeing him every day but I never kept another pet in the classroom. Biscuit became a legend in the school and the jokes about how to get rid of a class inspector by using a gerbil have never gone away.

Chapter Four

'Whose pigs are these, whose pigs are these, they are John Potts and
   they're covered in spots, whose pigs are these?'

A famous rhyme sang at Kentwell, the Tudor recreation centre in Long Melford, Suffolk. And without doubt it was the best day visit we ever made. It really was a wonderful experience for pupils and staff alike. Kentwell in the eighties was open for about four weeks during June and July every year. We took mainly year 8s, visiting also Long Melford church and the high street with its quaint little tea and antique shops. And, the journey there took us through quintessential English villages like Clare and Cavendish. But it was no doubt that Kentwell stole the show. On arrival, we would queue up outside in groups with other schools until our guide took us through the canvas time tunnel back into the chosen Tudor or Stuart year.

The actors lived in tents on the field for the duration of the event and they dressed accordingly to their position in society, either very rich nobles who were mainly located near or inside the mansion or peasants who worked in the fields. On one of the first visits we were met by a young lady who approached some of the boys and held out a pot and asked in a very rural accent 'Do you want to p.....s in my pot?' As you can imagine the kids were quite shocked to hear this but the woman went on to explain that urine was often used to wash clothes which helped get them clean. We were given a demonstration as she washed and scrubbed clothes in the stream, although I'm certain she didn't actually use real urine! It was moments like this that made Kentwell such a fabulous place to visit. The actors all had their own characters and were very convincing in their role, And what's more our students were encouraged to join in the activities. Outside they would be given a hoe and told to weed the fields, or plant seeds in the garden. Many were also given the chance to to have a go at archery and some volunteers were even put in the stocks. And there was always the aroma of wood burning fires, which added to the atmosphere. Inside the mansion we would be introduced to the Lord and Lady of the house, we would watch Tudor dancing with authentic music and instruments, often being invited to take part. Sometimes, depending on the political situation of the chosen time period, we would be quizzed about our loyalty to the King and threatened with arrest if they detected traitors!

In the kitchen, the servants would show us the types of food they were preparing for the nobles on that day. The students loved it as they could join in so many activities and really experience what it was like to live and work in Tudor England. And the actors were brilliant, completely ignoring modern day questions, focusing on their role and patiently demonstrating their skills.

During the eighties, we made an annual trip to Kentwell, although it was so popular that many primary school children visited the site and often dressed up in Tudor garments, which was fun for them but over the years I felt it lost its impact and unique appeal for our age groups as so many pupils had already visited Kentwell already at a much younger age.

There was only one occasion where a Kentwell visit ended in disappointment and acrimony. Our group had been visiting the Tudor kitchen where the staff were cutting up vegetables and making pastry for the pies, As we left to move on to the next display area one of the servants in the kitchen caught me up and mumbled something along the lines of

'Methinks a crime has been committed and a highly valuable utensil has gone missing, and methinks the villain may be secreting the object on his person amongst your merry band.' At first I thought it was a joke, another role play for us to enjoy. But I soon realised he was serious. A valuable Tudor knife was missing from the kitchen table and he assumed someone in our party was responsible. I asked him had he seen anyone take the knife and once again he started with 'methinks the said object it has disappeared and..' at that point I interrupted and told him to stop speaking in that stupid way, saying this isn't role play and you are accusing one of our students of stealing the knife. I got the group together and asked if anyone had seen the knife or 'picked it up by mistake.' No-one owned up or knew anything and I felt the pupils were telling the truth. The rest of the day was rather soured after that incident which was a shame.

In the earlier days of the seventies the only history trip was a visit to Castle Acre and Castle Rising where the students drew pictures of castle walls and visited the old monastery. Later on, apart from Kentwell, I also arranged visits for yr 8s to visit HMS Belfast and then the London Dungeons, recently opened in Tooley Street, close to London Bridge. Some thought it was a brilliant place, with its gory exhibits of imprisonment and torture but others, both students and parents, felt it was not suitable for young children. I did accept this so we looked for other suitable venues,

Apart from Kentwell, my other favourite history day trip was to York. It was a long day, nearly 200 miles from Sawston, but with an early start we were in York within three hours. The cathedral is magnificent and I usually managed to get a group booking for Jorvik on the site of an old Viking settlement, where a carriage takes you on a ride through an authentic Viking village, surrounded with the sights and sounds of life from a thousand years ago. However, on one occasion in 1984 our coach was stopped by police as we approached Yorkshire. This was at the time of the Miners Strike led by Arthur Scargill. Pickets were being bussed around to various locations to support local miners who were on strike. Government legislation banned the so called Flying Pickets and vast numbers of police blocked main roads and searched vehicles if they suspected pickets were on the move in vans and coaches. The police actually bordered our coach and after a cursory look around we were allowed to continue our journey. A sign of the times but it was an interesting experience for our students to view first hand another part of the country caught up in this bitter dispute.

I have focused here on mainly history trips but there were other trips I was involved in, especially once the London Eye arrived. This was a spectacular highlight for a visit to London once Activities week became a regular and enjoyable part of the school calendar during the summer term. Ironically the London Eye is situated almost next to the current South Bank site of the London Dungeons, now housed in what used to be County Hall. Our Lower school secretary, Kay Molloy, organised the West End activities week visits to London, where in addition to the Eye we had a picnic in the park and saw the House of Commons, Big Ben and Buckingham Palace.

There were also trips to Stansted Mounfitchet and the toy museum next door. Once we we were able to drive alongside the runway of Stansted airport and watch the fire brigade on a training exercise.

The great thing about activities week is that we tried to ensure that all pupils who were not on residential visits that week got at least one trip out. This I think is still the case.

Oh and we never did find the Kentwell knife or John Potts' pigs!

Chapter Five

Birds and the Bees, Wasps, Spiders and Monkees

The gulls came every year, you could rely on them almost to the day. Around the middle of October they would arrive, at last fifty of them, and make their winter quarters at the college, mainly sitting on the roof of the Lower school Hall waiting for a handout. They were particularly in evidence around break time and as soon as the pupils had gone in, down the gulls swooped into the playground, fighting and shrieking, looking for pieces of discarded food. At the end of the day when Elvis went round to collect the rubbish bins they would be waiting for him, looking down from the roof. We all called him Elvis on account of his jet black hair, he must have been getting on for eighty but came every day, a really friendly man. He would take out any discarded food and throw it on the ground, seconds later he would be surrounded by high pitched shrills of the gulls polishing off what the kids had left behind. The gulls did a great job in helping to recycle wasted food. Some people refer to them as flying rats but I love the sea gulls, they always remind me of the coast, or just gulls as Terry Saunders told me, 'no such thing as a seagull,' he said, only different types of gull. I know they can be quite aggressive in some places but they kept their distance at Sawston and although they got close I never saw them take anything out of anyone's hands or lunch box.

I admit whenever I was out on playground duty I would always buy one of the delicious, warm sausage rolls from the canteen and throw a few pieces down for the gulls. I think our Principal at the time, June Cannie, noticed this for she sent round a message on the daily bulletin forbidding people from feeding the gulls at break time! But by mid-March they had all had gone to their new summer breeding grounds before returning again in the autumn.

Apart from the gulls, we had very few problems with other birds, occasional pigeons that got into the building but somehow managed to find a way out again. On one occasion someone found an injured bird on the path and we put it in a box and took it to the biology lab, but it didn't survive. In addition to the gulls, the squirrels were often evident swinging in the branches, particularly around the old English mobiles near the Lower school office. Some squirrels in certain places can become tame and take food from your hand, especially if they are used to friendly tourists. I've noticed this and fed them myself in and around St James' Park in London, also in the grounds of the Abbey at Bury St Edmunds. But at Sawston they kept their distance. And then something strange happened, they all disappeared, There were rumours, always denied by the site manager, that pest control had been called in to get rid of them. They could have just moved on to another area I suppose, I don't know if they have returned to the college since.

I am calling this chapter birds and bees but I think it should read birds and wasps, because bees rarely entered the classroom, mostly visible around the flower beds outside the main hall and the language block. But wasps, they are a very different species. I used to dread that time in September, a warm sunny day when a wasp, drunk on sweet liquids, buzzes into the classroom, flying in that slow, aimless way, skimming over thirty heads and desks trying to find somewhere to land. As the teacher, you see it fly in and, of course, it doesn't go out again. Five seconds later the first student spots it and screams in terror. 'Ah Wasp Wasp!' or jasper as we used to call them. Then there's the next stage where someone will grab a ruler and start chasing it around, swinging his ruler in thin air, trying to squash it or flick it out of the window and if the ruler does connect it's more likely to land on someone's desk rather than go out of the window, which means more squeals and disruption. Always a pain at that time of the year. It may be just me but there doesn't seem to be so many wasps around these days as there used to be but if one ever does come into a classroom with his nasty little sting you know he's going to cause pandemonium. At home I don't take a lot of notice of wasps, or else I'll get a piece of card and a glass and try and capture it and send it on its way. That's not really practical in the classroom but I always tried to encourage students not to kill living things either inside or outside. Not just wasps. For lurking in the cupboards or in the dark corners of the room are the spiders, perfectly harmless unless you're teaching in the Australian outback. My view is always the same, ignore them, leave them alone and they will rarely bother you.

But I did have one incident when I was actually on supply teaching at Linton Village College. I was supervising a class of year nines in the library and resources base, when there was an almighty scream from a girl in the balcony area above. It really was piercing, A spider had run under the desk. Now I do appreciate that some people have real phobias about spiders but what annoyed most was this girl was chasing this spider and hammering the poor thing with a book, while still squealing. Then again, we're all different.

I once demonstrated to my grandson at a party outside in his garden how to capture a wasp using a glass and a piece of cardboard. Then keeping the card in place take the wasp outside or down the bottom of the garden and let it go. Problem solved. Or in this case it wasn't, for the moment I sat down again I felt something crawling on the back of my neck. It was a wasp and it stung me. Kind of reverse karma! Was it the same wasp? I'll never know!

One morning the secretary phoned me to say there was a new family arrived whose daughters may be joining the school, and they wanted a tour. I was free at the time and so I picked up the file. It was a family called Dolenz. I remember joking 'It's not Micky Dolenz from the Monkees is it?' The record file stated Los Angeles. I was still like 'No Way!' But it really was. Only mum came for the tour with the girls, she herself a former model called Tina Dow. They were living in Cambridge and she said that Micky visited frequently but spent his time working in California. The girls all came to the college, Charlotte was the eldest, then Emily,and in my year group, Georgia. Charlotte actually acted in my play *Performing Rights* and got quite friendly with my son, Chris. In fact I recall taking him to a party at their house in Hills Road, when Micky was staying. When Georgia was in year 10 she decided to take her work experience with her dad's music and video company back in the states. I did ask whether I would be allowed to visit to check on her progress but the answer was no!

But one day after school there was a knock on my office door, I opened it and standing there was Charlotte with her dad, Micky, asking whether I could show him around the school. He was a really nice guy, very friendly. I told him in the Sixties my wife was a big fan and we still had a copy of their LP. The last I heard Micky is still working in music production, and so is Georgia, in California. Not sure about the others but they were such nice girls with an amazing background!

Chapter Six

Snakes Alive

I have a pet snake, a Royal python called Monty, who is twenty five years old, very good age for this breed of python although the eldest royal python in captivity lived to the great age of 49 years!
When people ask me his name, they always respond with 'Ah, Monty Python,' named after the sixties TV show, to which I always reply 'Oh no, he's named after Montezuma, the Aztec Emperor!' They always look a bit bemused when they hear that. He was a Christmas present from my sons in 1998, he wasn't wrapped up though! He was a tiny little hatchling, and grew quite quickly, feeding on frozen tiny mice. But after a few months he refused to take his food. On two occasions I had to take him back to Lorna, the owner of the shop where he was purchased, where she was able to keep him for a few days and get him to strike at his food. But it never worked for me and for a year or so I had the unpleasant task of force feeding him, which was stressful for Monty, 'There's no alternative, otherwise he will die,' said Lorna.

So I had to continue with force feeding, until on one occasion he took it voluntarily and since then for the last twenty years he has taken his mouse on his own. He still goes through occasional periods where he doesn't eat, sometimes for weeks which can be frustrating. But this reluctance is a common problem with Royals, which is a shame because apart from eating they are very chilled snakes, beautiful to look at and easy to handle. Mike Butcher a Maths teacher in my year team, bought one for his family but unfortunately the constant problems with not eating led to Mike reluctantly giving him away.

I was introduced to this beautiful breed of snake by Tom Lawton, a year 8 student at the time, who occasionally brought in his own collection of snakes for showing in assemblies. Actually it was his mum who brought them in. She didn't mind handling them at all but when I first saw a Royal python I knew that was the snake I wanted. Tom would come round and advise on the progress of our other snakes. Shane initially kept a garter snake, a very thin and lively little snake who could give you a nip. Following this Shane bought a corn snake, lovely markings and very gentle although often when he was handled he had a habit of pooping all over your hand and arm. Our corn snake lived quite happily with Monty in the same cage without any problem. A neighbour of mine, Marina, a pupil at the college, also had a corn snake as a pet when she was about 14. I looked after her corn snake on a couple of times when her family were away but he wasn't so friendly and would often try and bite you. Showing again, how unpredictable snakes can be in their temperament and behaviour, even if they are of the same breed.

But there was nothing quite like the Californian King Snake that Christopher bought as his own. We wanted him to have a hatchling, because they get used to being handled from a very young age. She was already eighteen months old when we purchased her, and not used to being handled. Even when trying to change its water she would fly across the cage and attempt to bite It was a nasty, aggressive snake, it bit Chris a few times. Then Chris went off to Uni, Shane had already left home so I was given the task of looking after the King. And there was no way she would ever live in the same cage as Monty. The King would get into a feeding frenzy when detecting a meal. Strangely enough, once she was out of the cage she was quite calm and would let anyone handle her, she loved slithering across the floor of my office and didn't mind being picked up. But once back in her cage, she was something else. In fact, Tom came round a couple of times, he picked her out of her cage and gave me some advice on how to handle her. It was not something I wanted to do regularly! The King snake lived to about 18 years of age before she died, leaving me with just Monty.

After leaving school Tom continued his interest and great love of snakes and applied successfully to work as a a keeper at the world famous Australian Zoo near Brisbane, owned by the legendary Steve Irwin. Very rare for someone to have that opportunity, and I think Sawston can be very proud of Tom's knowledge and achievements. Tom probably has his own reptile house somewhere now!

Monty has history and in Sawston he's quite famous. When I was Head of Year I took him into assembly on several occasions to meet the pupils, and also organised 'meet and great sessions' at youth activities in the evenings at the Marven Centre. He was featured in the local magazine and also became the star of a classroom drama production in RE. The Year 8s wrote their own scripts about the Garden of Eden, mainly featuring Adam and Eve. We even had a serpent played, of course, by Monty. I did the voice over and pretended to be the tree of knowledge.

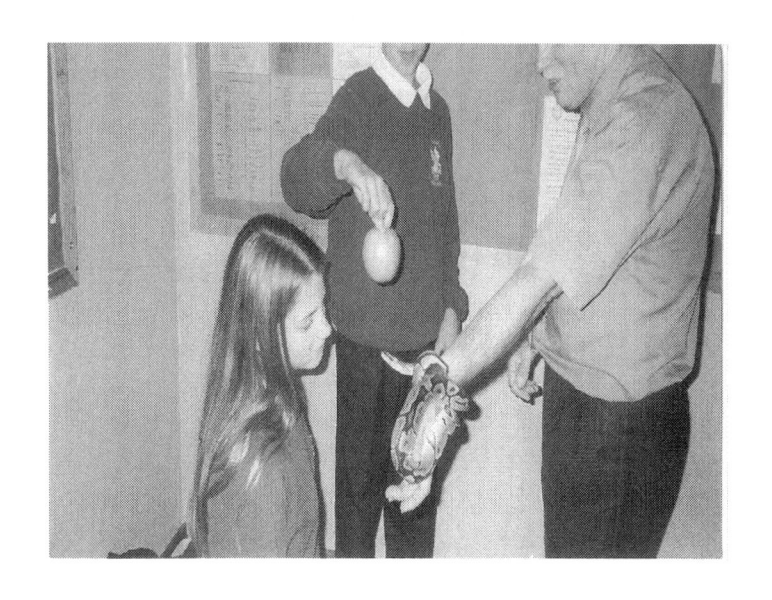

MONTY'S STARRING ROLE

A photograph shows a Year 8 pupil, Rachel Clark (Pilsworth) playing Eve and talking with Monty. She liked him so much that she developed an interest in snakes and later decided to get one of her own.

Monty is a very gentle snake, easy to handle. Usually I find that most people are very curious about snakes so bringing Monty in to school gave students a chance to hold him and ask questions. I always kept Monty at a distance and only allowed those who were confident enough and those I knew I could trust to hold him on their own. I do understand some people have phobias about snakes. Our Lower school secretary Kay Molloy, is terrified of snakes, if she knew I was bringing Monty into assembly she would run out of the office, she couldn't even look at him! On a Year 11 school trip to Disneyland Paris Kay took some of the students into a virtual 3D cinema experiences. Unfortunately this particular film featured a snake with fangs bursting through the screen and striking at the audience. Kay left very quickly!

However, with patience and care, you can persuade people to touch and handle snakes. Invariably, they expect a snake to be slimy and are surprised at the dry skin and how beautiful the patterns and colours can be close up. Mel, our lovely catering manager at Sawston for several years and a friend of Sue's, came over one afternoon and as we were chatting she said she had this phobia about snakes. I took Monty out of the cage. She agreed she would look at him from a distance but gradually she became more curious, and managed a light touch. I finally persuaded her to hold him on her lap. Mel was so excited that we took a photograph which she sent to her partner Nick, as she was so pleased she had over come her fear of snakes.

I am always happy to introduce Monty to anyone, he's a very chilled snake and quite used to being handled. My two granddaughters, Madeleine and Florence, love him and Joel, my grandson, always asks about him.

Chapter Seven

Another Brick In the Wall

My days at the High school

In 1965 I joined the Cambridge Labour Party Young Socialists. I had always been interested in politics, encouraged by my maternal grandfather, John Creek, who spent all his life working on the railways. Not surprisingly he was a solid Labour man and l was influenced by the Labour Government elected in 1964 with its emphasis on change and modernisation. Of course this was also the time of the Swinging Sixties and like a lot of teenagers I was influenced by the ideas, the music and the fashion of the time with its emphasis on youth. In fact, one of the best days of my life was seeing my heroes, The Beatles, perform live on stage in Cambridge in 1963 at the Regal.

During my time in the young socialists I canvassed during elections, visited the House of Commons and met some very interesting politicians. Bessie Braddock, the Labour MP for Liverpool Exchange, visited Cambridge on one occasion and came to the Labour Party hall in Norfolk street, where she made us all a cup of tea. I was quite left wing in those days, influenced by our Labour MP, Robert Davies, who often came to local meetings when he wasn't in the Commons. Sadly, he died just a few months after being elected in 1966. During a public meeting in Cambridge I criticised the Labour Foreign secretary, George Brown, for supporting the American bombing of Hanoi during the Vietnam conflict. When he started to answer, I shook my head in disagreement to which a rather irate Brown yelled from the platform 'Don't you shake your head at me! Listen to what I'm saying!' I actually quite liked George Brown, he was a colourful and controversial character. I was very against the American involvement in Vietnam and like many sixteen year olds, very idealistic, seeing things in black and white and convinced that we were the future. The Vietnam conflict has long been forgotten but I can appreciate how strong feelings are today amongst young people, particularly on issues like mental health and climate change. However, I was shocked when The Prime Minister, Harold Wilson,visited Cambridge in 1966, and I was a steward on duty. I recall looking out of a window on to the street below as a large hostile crowd surged around Wilson's car as it pulled alongside the Guildhall. Protesters hammered on the roof of the car and police fought to control the violent mob. Eventually Wilson was bundled through a side door but one policemen was knocked to the ground and sustained a broken leg, the Officer never worked again.

After the weekly Labour Party meetings we often adjourned to the Man on the Moon public house in Norfolk Street. One evening I was sitting with a very committed Socialist and local teacher, Mary, when her son Roger came in to join us. He was a few years older than me and it turned out that he was also a student at the Cambridgeshire High school, where I was educated, which he hated. We had something in common there. Roger bought me a lager and we chatted about some of the awful teachers and the elitist system in the high school. He told me that his passion was music and he was a member of a pop group hoping to make a breakthrough on the music scene. I asked him jokingly if he could use a drummer or a vocalist in his band. I only saw him once more as I think he moved to London to pursue a music career. A few months later, in 1967 Roger Water's group released its début single just getting into the Top twenty, which was quite an achievement. But it was the second song which blew me away. It was released in the summer of 1967. The song was called *See Emily Play* written by Syd Barrett, who was also at my school, and the group was called PINK FLOYD. By this time Barrett was lead guitarist and lead singer. Sadly his time was very limited and he left the group in 1969 after excessive drug taking and suffering a mental breakdown and despite a couple of failed comeback attempts, he returned to Cambridge and became a recluse, dying of cancer in 2006.

Pink Floyd went on to become one of the greatest groups in the world, especially after the definitive *Dark Side of the Moon*, released in 1975, with most or all lyrics written by Roger Waters. I didn't get to sing in the band but I did occasionally use their songs and lyrics at Sawston. And the best example was '*Another Brick in the Wall*' from the album *The Wall*. I played the song in assembly several times and used the lyrics in PSE and English lessons, with its emphasis on teachers' dark sarcasm and control in the classroom, 'leave those kids alone'. This song was written by Roger and reflected his time at the Cambridgeshire High School where he was unhappy, saying in an interview 'I hated every second of it, apart from games. The regime at school was a very oppressive one ... the same kids who are susceptible to bullying by other kids are also susceptible to bullying by the teachers.'

So was the school really that bad? Oh yes.

It's a great song but I took the opposite view. Yes in most schools children follow a similar timetable throughout, wear the same uniform and are bound by the same rules. Children are not just educational bricks in the wall. In PSE lessons we used templates to colour in the bricks and annotate key words that reflected the skills and individuality of each pupil. I think Roger would be pleased with that. After all, each brick is just as important as another in a building. The curriculum gives everyone the opportunity to study core subjects such as Maths, Science and English plus the options to develop and specialise in other subjects from Year 9 or

Year 10 onwards.

Liam Gallagher left school at fifteen with few qualifications and a damning report that basically said he would amount to nothing. He became one of the greatest vocalists during the Nineties with his band Oasis, a millionaire several times over and still recording solo albums. School presumably did little to inspire Liam, which is sad. When I was training to be a teacher I lived near Southgate tube station. In nearby affluent Winchmore Hill there was Broad Lane, full of stunning detached houses with electronic gates. A friend told me about a man who lived in one of these houses who left school unable to read or write. But he built up a business as a scrap metal merchant and became a millionaire. Occasionally he could be seen cruising around the locality in a powder blue Rolls Royce. However, people like the scrap metal dealer and Liam Gallagher are the exceptions. I suspect though that Roger Waters was aiming more at the quality of teaching (or lack of it) than the subjects on offer. But was he right about the teachers at the Cambridgeshire High School?

I passed the eleven plus in 1961 and started in September at the High school. I vividly remember the first day, cycling up to the main gate. I carried a satchel on my back and in the basket at the front an enormous, flapping brown paper bag containing my PE kit and rugby kit, not knowing whether I would need all this on the first day.

The school was a very different environment to the local Brunswick Primary school. But I made friends and settled in quite well, although I found some of the work difficult, especially algebra which I didn't understand. The only problem I encountered during the first year was being caught by a sixth form prefect playing 'tig' with others in the school building during the lunch hour, which was out of bounds. The prefect called Francis, hit me and my friend, across the back of the head as we were ordered down the stairs. I had a headache for the rest of the day. I complained at home and Dad wrote a letter of complaint to the headmaster. The next day I was called in to his office, and told off for breaking the school rules. However, the head did write a reply to my dad saying although I was in the wrong 'in a part of the building where he had no business to be' the Prefect had no right to hit me, and this issue would be dealt with. I still have a copy of the letter. I never heard any more so whether the issue was ever properly dealt with I don't know.

After making reasonable progress in the first year, the second year was a disaster. I was finding the work more difficult. At primary school I was usually in the top five of the class for most subjects, but now I was in the third or bottom set for most subjects, with little or no opportunity to move up. I didn't help myself, I was quite lazy and started leaving my books at school to avoid doing homework. After two such occasions in geography, I was given a two hour Saturday morning detention by the teacher Mr Bryan, the first person in my form to be given a Saturday as it was known. Worse was to come. Twice a term the Diligence lists were published, where pupils were given grades for effort in every subject. The grades ranged from A=Very Good to E=Very bad. I recall a boy from another class stopping me in the corridor and announcing in his loudest voice 'You got five Ds!'   Five Ds, it was the worst diligence result in my year. In school assembly the headmaster solemnly read out the names of all pupils who were commended for achieving two A grades, and then all the names of pupils who recorded 2 Ds or more, including me with the worst result, which resulted in another Saturday detention. It was quite humiliating, although I tried to laugh it off with my friends afterwards.

I don't know why I didn't work or try. No one, least of all my Form teacher, Mr Fielder, took me aside and asked if everything was OK or gave me advice or support. No, all he did was complain and reprimand me for being lazy and letting the whole form down. I hated him. He was our music teacher and for homework we were given an assignment to research a famous composer and then present the work in class. My composer was Sibelius. In the next music lesson I was called up first. I didn't mind because I had actually written two sides on listing his achievements and looked forward to sharing my knowledge with the rest of class, and proving Fielder wrong. It was a disaster. My opening line was 'Sibelius studied music at university in Helsinki, Finland,' but unfortunately I pronounced the name as 'Helenski'. That was as far as I got. Fielder berated me in front of the class, 'typical of you Reynolds, haven't even bothered to get the name right, why I expected anything else,from you I don't know...etc, etc sit down until you can get it right.' I was more angry than upset. The next diligence list was due out in a few days. This time I got 3 Ds and another Saturday detention, and the usual form reprimand. I actually protested 'but I've improved Sir and only get three Ds this time.' It didn't make any difference, I went home and told my parents I wanted to leave the High school and transfer to the local Secondary Modern instead, where the work would be easier, I thought. My parents were sympathetic, Dad made an appointment to see my Form Tutor to ask if this was possible, but Mr Fielder told him that I needed to stay at the high school, it would be a disaster to move. He also said that my problem was lack of structure as well as lack of effort but my behaviour was good. Um, something positive at last. My parents were advised to check my homework and make sure that I finished all the tasks properly. Interesting that all the responsibility was on my parents and me. I didn't have a homework report and no teacher checked on my progress at school. But it did actually work up to a point. There was some improvement in my effort, I still found science and Maths very hard but the number of Ds reduced which was something. But I turned a corner that year largely due to one teacher, Peter Bryan, the teacher who gave me my first Saturday detention. After my initial problems with homework in Geography I began to settle down and enjoy the subject. On one occasion he asked where does most of our sugar come from? I was the only pupil to put my hand up, 'West Indies?'

'Good,' said Mr Bryan, 'do you know which island?'

I did know. 'Cuba.'

'Excellent, well done Reynolds.' And that was the turning point for me with Mr Bryan and Geography. A rare moment of praise but it really helped motivate me and improved my relationship with him. Within a year I rose to the top of class both in term work and examinations. This was a standard I maintained until I left the High school with a view to becoming either a geography or a history teacher, When there was no room in the A level Geography class at the Arts and Technology college, I settled for history but ended up teaching geography as well at Sawston. Early on in my teaching career Peter Bryan, in his new role as Sixth Form co-ordinator for the county, visited Sawston for a meeting. It was good to shake hands with him and thank him for inspiring me to become a teacher. He won my respect but many other teachers at the high school didn't.

It was a very narrow, highly academic and elitist education. There was no doubt that many of the staff knew their subjects, the majority had Oxbridge degrees, but only a few were capable of teaching their subject in an interesting and informative way. Most lessons were 'talk and chalk'. The teachers wrote on the blackboard, the pupils copied down the notes in their rough note books and then copied up the rough notes in best in their exercise books for homework. There was little or no class support for pupils in any subject. The philosophy was basically 'sink or swim.' I was placed in the C stream from the first year and remained there for most subjects for five years. Some of the staff, but not all, could be patronising and snobbish in their attitude. The physics teacher, Mr Bullman, never smiled or made a joke in class, He talked in a strange kind of whisper, referring to physics as 'fuzzicks'. If anyone made a mistake, it was also because we were in the 'C stream' not like the clever intelligent A grade boys, and didn't deserve a place in a grammar school, implying we were all too stupid and should be in a secondary modern school. 'If you're the cream, God knows what the milk is like,' was another example of the attitude towards lower ability and secondary modern pupils.

One teacher I detested in the Third Year was Eric 'whacker' Warne, he taught me history, a subject that I liked. Although he kept a slipper on the corner of his desk in class, I don't recall him actually whacking people in class but he was sarcastic and unpleasant. It was rule by intimidation. If any student asked a question in class or even ventured a creative explanation of any event, Warne would stop the boy speaking, especially if they used the expression but 'Sir I thought..'

'You don't think boy you had a silly notion.' He would get quite nasty if you disagreed or refused to utter the phrase 'I'm sorry Sir, I had a silly notion.' Absolute idiot. Most of the time I kept my head down and didn't answer questions in class after being ridiculed on a couple of occasions. My marks were average to good. I fell out with Mr Warne though big time over Mary Queen of Scots. We were set a homework to write an essay on the main events of Mary's life. I was quite interested in this topic and wrote three pages and was very pleased with my effort. I expected a good mark but when the books were returned, mine was held up by Mr Warne who informed the class that I had only scored one mark out of ten, because I had written about the life of Mary Queen of Scots, and it should have been on the life of Mary Tudor. I apologised and I was ordered to write the essay again using the right Mary, which I did, but he refused to change my mark. Two weeks later, the Diligence Lists were issued for each class. I knew I had been working steadily in most subjects averaging B and Satisfactory C grades for everything. I was shocked when I saw my history grade. It was an E, Very bad. which meant an automatic Saturday morning detention. Most of my mates in class told our Form Master this was really unfair and I didn't deserve an E. After all, diligence grades were supposed to be about effort over the term. Yes, I had made a bad mistake with one homework but I had worked well in most lessons and always completed my homework on time. My form teacher, Mr Bilton, was sympathetic, and said he would speak to Mr Warne and I should come to the staff room at break time. I was hoping that maybe the grade could be changed. I waited outside and the door opened. I could just about see the silver coffee pots through the thick fug of tobacco smoke. A very irate Mr Warne appeared in the doorway. Before I had any chance to say anything, he asked 'How many marks did you get for your Mary essay?'

'One Sir but I..'

'One mark. That' s why you got an E so don't come crying to me.' Then he slammed the door and went back inside the staff room, probably to rant at my Form master for questioning his judgement. I certainly wasn't crying but I was very angry. I never forgot that incident. And I vowed that if I ever became a teacher I would never speak to pupils in that way or humiliate them in front of everyone in class or assembly. Another word that came to mind later was justice. But I did manage to get my own back on Mr Warne a few years later. It was in the early seventies, major changes were taking place in education in Cambridgeshire. The eleven plus was being phased out, grammar schools were to be abolished and all children over the age of eleven would be educated in the local comprehensive school. By this time I was training to be a teacher and fully supported the new educational system. The local newspaper gave a lot of coverage to the plan. And then I saw it. A letter from Eric Warne, a high school history master, totally opposed to comprehensive schools which in his view would be totally detrimental, preventing the bright children from getting a proper academic education and lowering standards for everyone. I took great delight in writing a reply to the Cambridge News stating what my education was like at the High school and that Mr Warne was part of an elitist system, which was unfair to the majority of children who were separated at the age of eleven. I never saw any other letters from him but he failed to stop comprehensive education and in 1974 the High school became Hills road Sixth form college. Mr Warne, I heard, died soon afterwards. But amazingly something happened a few years later when I was teaching history. It was almost as though Eric Warne returned from the grave to help one of my students to pass her 'O' level history.

One day in the seventies I was invigilating a history O level examination. I taught one of the groups. As I was walking up and down between the rows of students, I glanced at one girl's paper. She was answering a question on Queen Mary Tudor but unfortunately to my horror I saw that she was writing about Mary Queen of Scots and she had already written the first paragraph on the wrong Queen! Just like I did once. Juliet looked up, saw my expression and immediately crossed out the paragraph and wrote Mary Tudor instead...then glanced up again. Of course I couldn't say or do anything but she got the message. Juliet nodded and smiled. She passed the examination and I believe, became a teacher. So I have to say 'thank you Eric, I forgive you, you came good in the end!'

At Sawston I don't recall having a nickname or if I did I never heard about it. When I arrived at the college in 1975 there was another teacher called Reynolds, Paul Reynolds who was the Head of Middle school. He was bigger than me so I was known as 'little Mr Reynolds' while he was 'big Mr Reynolds.' To my knowledge no other members of staff had nicknames. But at the High School it was different, a tradition that had been around for many years. 'Whacker' Warne was one example. But there were others, some of which pupils themselves had no idea where they came from. The Headmaster was known as 'Beak', a science teacher was known as 'Boxer' Mills' after Freddie Mills, the boxer. The deputy Head was known as 'George', his first name, others included 'Rubber guts', 'Snot', 'Gach' after his initials, and Moses Watson, and 'Mutt' my Form teacher in the last year. I don't know why.

At the start of every lesson, one boy would always be stationed in the doorway while the rest of us messed about and when the teacher was coming the lookout would yell 'Satch is coming' and we would hurtle back to our places before the teacher got into the classroom.

One day when I went to find my friend Paul in the class next door, a boy blocked my way and refused to let me through. I'm not sure how this was resolved but the boy in question was *Martin Amis,* later to become a famous novelist, I don't think he had a very happy time at the High school. I did read a few of his books later on when he became famous but I doubt he read any of mine!

I have to say that not all the High School teachers were bad. The head of English. Mr Walker, run a drama club which I belonged to which was fun. Mr Barlow, my history teacher, encouraged my interest in politics, and Barry Williams, a young English teacher, inspired me to study English literature. But it's fair to say teachers who were inspirational, or showed great enthusiasm for the subject and actually enjoyed teaching children were few and far between in my school. The lessons I really learned at High School helped form my own philosophy as a teacher in later years. I would never be like them.

Roger Waters told *Mojo*, in December 2009, that his song is meant to be satirical. He explained: "You couldn't find anybody in the world more pro-education than me. But the education I went through in boys' grammar school in the '50s was very controlling and demanded rebellion. The teachers were weak and therefore easy targets.'

I rather hope Roger gets to read this. I owe him a drink!I

Chapter Eight

Roland and the Rats from 2B. 1984

'Never work with Children or Animals'
Katy Murray, Author and Physiotherapist told me
recently

A wet and dismal November day, lunchtime duty in the playground. Most of the pupils huddle in corners or try to reach one of the classrooms which they are not allowed in during break times. The regulation was eventually changed but I guess it harks back to the Victorian idea that fresh air and exercise was very good for growing children, whatever the time of the year. But it was also because it was easier to put everyone outside where you only need a couple of supervisors. During the summer months the school field is open at break times and duty can be very pleasant as most of the kids sit around chatting in small groups. But it doesn't matter whether it's ten degrees below freezing or if there's a hurricane blowing, you can always guarantee the small group of dedicated footballers, mostly boys, will be out on the playground.

On this particular day, I get a message from the office. Central Television are on the telephone and want to speak to me and it's important. I have no idea what they want. A lady called Sheila Ford tells me she is calling about a children's programme called The Saturday Show, that is broadcast on ITV every week. The show, hosted by Tommy Boyd and Isla St Clare, is a mixture of cartoons, pop songs and celebrity guests. And long before Britain's Got Talent hit our screens, the Saturday Show featured a regular slot called 'Talented Teachers'. At this point, I still had no idea what this had got to do with me until Sheila explained that three of my first years had written to the programme, without my knowledge, saying that I was always singing at school and that I would make a good competitor for the programme. And would I like to come up to the studio in Birmingham with the girls for an audition?

I wouldn't really call it singing, more of a tuneless hum in the classroom and corridors, which many many people have commented on over the years. Rarely complimentary. I think Central TV must have been desperate for contestants!

Later that day, I found the three girls, Nicola Pulvertaft, Alison Brookes and Joanne Minks who looked a bit sheepish. 'Have you got something you want to tell me?'

I wasn't annoyed, I thought it sounded fun and the girls were excited that I had agreed to do the audition. I phoned all the parents and we arranged to visit the studio soon after Christmas. It was only then that I realised I hadn't got an act.

I decided not to sing but opted instead to do an impersonation of Roland Rat, the puppet, that according to all reports had saved ITV's Good Morning Britain. The programme, a mixture of news and serious interviews was haemorrhaging viewers and looked certain to be axed, until the company changed complete direction and introduced a children's section. Roland Rat became one of the most popular puppet figures of all time.

We set off very early in the morning to arrive at the Central studios in Birmingham. It was quite an experience to stand in the wings with the girls and watch a live show unfold, the girls were part of the studio audience. Steve Davis, the world snooker champion was the guest on the show that day. After the show, while the parents and children went off to lunch, I had to do my audition in front of the producers. I was quite anxious when Steve Davis said he wanted to stay and watch. But I stumbled through a very basic routine, a mixture of corny jokes and Roland impersonations. I was certain I wouldn't get any further. The Production team briefly conferred notes and then the Producer said. 'Kelvin, we'll write you a script. You are going to be on the show live!'

Steve Davis congratulated me. 'I can't do Roland Rat,' he joked.
'I can't play snooker!' I replied. Of course the girls leapt in the air with excitement when they realised that would also be appearing with me on live television.

It was snowing on the Friday evening in January when we all set off for Birmingham. Central TV were generous enough to pay for a hotel for everyone. Sue and my eldest son Shane, aged 6, also came with me. We travelled in Lesley Pulvertaft's car, as the snow became heavier. Later that evening I went for dinner at the Holiday Inn where I met the production team and was given the script to learn for my three minute slot. On the Saturday morning we arrived early at the Central studios and I had an opportunity to run through the script a couple of times. The studio was decorated with silver balloons and rainbow scenery, which looked fantastic in 1984! The adults went to the Green room to watch the show where they were joined by the star guest, the one and only David Essex! Also on the show was Matthew Corbett and Sooty. Meantime, I was having trouble persuading my six year old to join the studio audience, Shane was definitely having second thoughts and in fairness to him, all the other kids were eleven and over. A man suddenly came alongside and started talking to Shane, assuring him it would be all right. It took me a few seconds to realise it was Jimmy Greaves, one of the greatest strikers in English football and one of my dad's all time heroes. The equivalent of Harry Kane today. Jimmy, now retired from football, did a regular slot on the programme called Sporting Spotlight. Jimmy was so kind and supportive. But unfortunately it didn't work, Shane was determined not to go on the set and returned to the Green Room.

I then got ready. My costume consisted of a stripy jumper and a headpiece consisting of pink ears and a long, furry nose that was supposed to represent Roland. Standing in the wings I watched the show progress, noting how everything run like clockwork. All the items were timed to the second, and this being a programme on ITV, there were several breaks for the adverts. An hour after the show started a lady wearing headphones and carrying a clipboard positioned me behind a heavy purple curtain to await my cue. I could hear what was going but I couldn't see anything. Tommy Boyd introduced the Talented Teachers contest. 'Our first contestant today...is..Kelvin Reynolds from Sawston Village College, Cambridge and his sponsors are Nicola, Joanne and Alison from Class 1L. Welcome to the Show.' For the first time I began to feel very nervous. My mouth felt dry and my heart was beating furiously. I was on my own behind this curtain, with an exit door to the left. I knew three million people would be watching on live television and I really was tempted to make a run for it.

'And what's Kelvin going to do for us..?'

'He's going to do Roland Rat.....'

'Well we want to see him, let's welcome Kelvin Roland Rat Reynolds.'

The music started and the purple curtain was drawn aside as I stepped out towards a white mark on the studio floor. The studio lights were dazzling and I can recall standing right opposite David Essex who sat in the star chair in the middle of the audience. In front, a heavy camera with the red light on. Showtime! Somehow, I managed to get through the corny jokes written for me like 'why don't rats eat penguins?....Because they can't get the wrappers off.' Studio groans. And then I did impressions of Roland Rat impersonating other famous people like Roy Castle and Max Bygraves. I could see David laughing and I remember pointing it out to the audience. I finished with a bit of tap dancing, and lots

'Ere rat fans' in Roland's trademark nasal whine then suddenly it was over. But not quite over as the pupil panel selected from the audience were to comment and give votes. Isla St Clair, a lovely lady, remarked how very clever it was to do Roland impersonating others. Alas, her encouraging words didn't work on the panel, who were not impressed, comments like 'He got the voice right but that was about it... I liked his pink ears.' Next up, the second contestant called the Man in the Box who did a puppet routine to music set in a booth bit like Punch and Judy. I didn't think it was that good but the pupil panel from Banbury gave him higher marks and he was declared the winner. My three minute claim to fame was over. The girls were very disappointed and almost in tears. It was a very deflated ride back to Sawston but thanks to Central TV, we had a great day and they looked after us very well. An experience that none of us would forget.

For a time, I had to endure endless chants of' 'Rat fans eee' every time I started a lesson but gradually it was forgotten. This was back in the day before internet and YouTube, although I still have an old VHS tape of the show from 1984. And by the nineties Roland had faded from our TV screens forever. I did however, make two appearances wearing the Roland headgear Central TV gave me as a souvenir at local fund-raising events. This stopped abruptly when my next door neighbour asked me to do my act for her daughter's sixth birthday party, to be held in the garden. I climbed over the fence and went straight into my routine. Half a dozen angelic looking girls in their beautiful party dresses, licking ice cream cones, gathered round. Before I'd finished the first sentence one girl stepped forward and squashed her ice cream on my head. Suddenly, all ten excited, screaming little girls joined in. I leapt over the fence back into my own garden, in a state of shock. My neighbour was very apologetic as no one had expected such a reaction-least of all me. On that day I hung up my

Roland Rat outfit and never did any more appearances again. Occasionally pupils still ask me about Roland Rat, but that's only because their parents remember watching the act when they were at school, although their children haven't a clue who he was.

About two years later I was in my classroom tidying up after school when a breathless young first year burst through the door. It was Yuko, a Japanese girl who was in my year group but who I also taught English lessons to as a private tutor after school. Her mother worked for the Japanese embassy in London and Yuko was a very bright girl. Yuko was one of a number of pupils who looked after the rabbits after school. Usually up to three rabbits lived in an outdoor compound, with individual hutches, protected by wire and wooden fences. The rabbit run was located on the exterior wall of the Biology lab.

'Mr Reynolds,' she said, 'one of the gerbils from the Biology labs has escaped and he's in the rabbit hutch! Can you come and get him?'

Now, I knew that apart from my own classroom gerbil, there were other gerbils kept in the Biology labs but I couldn't understand how on earth a gerbil could escape from a classroom, run down a corridor, through the fire doors and end up climbing into a rabbit hutch. On reaching the rabbit compound, I climbed over the fence. I had a horrible feeling I was not going to find a gerbil. I very carefully opened the hutch. Fluff, a rather overweight grey rabbit with floppy ears, was munching quite happily on cabbage leaves. And feasting quite happily beside him was another animal, not the gerbil but a young rat!

Yuko didn't realise and still thought it was a gerbil! She couldn't understand why I didn't put my hand in the cage and pull out this 'gerbil' and return him to his rightful home in the biology wing. I closed the door and told her that I would tell the caretaker and the biology dept straight away. I thanked Yuko for telling me and promised it would be sorted out. By the next morning, three more rats were scuttling around on the grass in front of the hutches. The pest controllers were called in immediately. They discovered that the rats had entered the compound from an underground tunnel that started in the field a hundred metres away. The rat pack had found a very convenient new food store, and apparently the rabbits were quite happy to tolerate their new rodent invaders.

The pest controllers used poison to get rid of the rats, the rabbit compound was broken up and concreted over and the rabbits were re- homed. Unfortunately, it was decided that no more animals would be kept outside on the school site, bringing to an end a tradition that had started forty years previously.

I read recently about a school that keeps alpacas in a fenced off area on site, the pupils help to look after the animals, and the wool is sold for garments. Maybe one day animals like these will return to Sawston.

Nicola, Alson and Joanne

Chapter Nine

We don't care what The Weatherman say

February 2003

Parents' Evening was coming to an end in the Spicer wing. My appointments were completed. I stepped outside my classroom into the corridor, there were a few stragglers heading towards the English classrooms. English teachers always seemed to be the last to finish their appointments! Walking towards me was a man wearing a long black overcoat speckled grey, an unusual design I thought to myself. But as he got nearer it wasn't a pattern but large snow flakes on his coat. Glancing up through the glass roof of the Spicer wing I could see the snow swirling in the night sky. Sue and I had decided on a Chinese take away for our meal that night and I would pick it up on my way home, from our favourite Lotus House in the High street. But by the time I reached my car, a blizzard was blowing and heavy snow was swirling everywhere. I could hardly see through the windscreen. I just about managed to get home.

The M11 and A14 became gridlocked, roads became impassable. People were trapped inside their cars and rescue vehicles were unable to get through as thousands of cars and lorries ground to a halt. Hundreds of people in Cambridgeshire and Essex became stranded. Roads were closed and people who had left off work earlier in the afternoon were taking up to eight hours to get home. No surprise that the all schools including SVC were closed the next day. From then on , we did occasionally have snow days when the school was closed although we never experienced anything like the blizzard of 2003.

In the seventies the big problem seemed to be ice forming on the country roads and on the hill leading into Sawston, which prevented school buses and coaches getting through from our local villages. But the school was rarely, if ever closed, even when some teachers who lived outside the catchment area couldn't get to school. Local children from Sawston could still get to school and we used a revised timetable, putting groups together. Decades later more detailed weather forecasting and regular gritting of the roads ensured that as far as possible we would never face conditions like 2003, although schools were still often closed because of the dangers of ice and the risks of accidents, and also boilers breaking down. Ironically, many pupils wanted to come to school on snow days so they could make ice slides and have snowball fights, but that didn't happen very often.

In October 1987 the South and East of England experienced a great storm, the wind howled all night. I remember it well as my youngest son was only a few weeks old and still having night feeds. The power was off and we had planned a seventh birthday party for Christopher. I actually walked to school that day although I assumed that it wouldn't be open. It was even dangerous to step outside the front door, let alone open the school. It was our first closure due to high winds. The wind picked up litter bins and hurled them across the playground.

Although it wasn't the same day I recall another whirlwind a few years later that erupted without warning one lunchtime. As the strength of the wind increased we decided to get everyone back inside the building. I was on duty that day and the area seemed clear when I noticed a little year seven huddled up against a wall outside. I ran over to her and said 'We need to get inside now!' We only just made it. A few seconds later a freak gust uprooted a small green house, the glass and metal frame took off, hurtled through the air and smashed into the wall in the exact spot where the girl and I had been standing seconds before, missing us by about three feet. Fortunately we reached safety. Another ten seconds I doubt whether either of us would have survived.

In the summer our block became very hot during heatwaves. There was no air conditioning, and leaving the exit doors in the block open had little or no effect on the pressure cooker classrooms. On one occasion it was so hot that I stopped teaching halfway through the lesson as we were all wilting. Maybe we have to think again about air conditioning in classrooms in the future, if as predicted, summers are likely to get hotter still.

But there's one overriding memory I have of freak weather conditions. The summer of 76, a heatwave that seemed to go on forever. It lasted all summer long, beautiful sunshine, hardly a cloud in the sky. But by July the heat was beginning to take its toll on the nation, Rivers, lakes and reservoirs dried up and many crops perished in the fields. Stand pipes were introduced in the streets in some areas and the Government created a special Minister for the Drought. And it was a very sticky, humid heat and very difficult to keep cool, especially at night. There was also the added risk of fires breaking out in such dry conditions. We lived in Hobart Road, off Mill Road in Cambridge at the time. I recall the blue flashing lights of the fire engines reflecting on the ceiling well after midnight, as they answered numerous emergency calls.

My classroom had lovely large windows but initially there were no blinds, and with the sun beating down continuously every day it was like being under a magnifying glass. The heat dominated the news every day. And there was no end to it. However, Jennifer Willis in my form and her friends discovered a special song that she taught us. A song which she claimed would make it rain. I'd never heard of it before. I don't know where it came from, I was told possibly from the indigenous tribes from North America. I can still remember the gist of it:

Commocoomarama..comoomaram vista oh oh commorama..vista .that's how it sounded to me and they worked out this little rain dance as well. It took a few weeks for the song to work! One day in September, the heavens opened at lunchtime, the rain was torrential but instead of coming in to shelter most of my crazy form and many other pupils remained in the playground and got absolutely drenched. I watched from the window, it was great see the sheer joy on their faces as they splashed around in the puddles and tasted rain for the first time in months.

The drought was over. We didn't know much about climate change in 1976, but the reservoirs slowly filled again and the harvest wasn't a complete disaster. Of course there have been extremely hot days since, both in the UK and other parts of the world. In fact Cambridge held the record for 4 years after recording the highest temperature ever in the UK, measured at the weather station in the Botanic Gardens in 2018.

But nothing will ever compare with that day when the clouds burst and Jenny and her friends said it was their song that made it happen.

In 1666, in his diary Samuel Pepys recorded that the 7th June was 'the hottest day ever than any one could remember.' Pepys was a very superstitious man, I'm sure he would have been delighted to promote 1R's rain song at the Royal court in London. And of course, sooner or later, it would have worked in the end!

Looking forward to a nice cop of coffee in peace until my Year 11 rabble took over. Actually, they're lovely really, well, most of the time...Flossie, Lauren,Zoe, Natalie..

Chapter Ten

The Ghost of Sawston Past

According to legend a dog known as Black Shuck haunts the Fens of East Anglia. The Beast has been seen on the footpath between Whittlesford and Sawston, although some say it may have been an escaped puma. There is no evidence to support either of these claims. In the centre of Sawston stands Sawston Hall built originally in 1517, and owned by the rich and powerful Catholic family, the Huddlestons. On certain nights it is said that the ghostly apparition of a grey lady glides across the lawns and driveway. The ghostly figure is thought to be that of Queen Mary Tudor, eldest daughter of Henry V111. After his death the King was succeeded by his legitimate heir, Edward, who was only nine years old at the time. The young boy King was controlled by powerful nobles like the Duke of Northumberland and persuaded to follow a strict Protestant religion that was imposed on the country. However, when Edward's health began to fail, Northumberland was worried that if he died he would be succeeded by his sister Mary, a devout Roman Catholic and next in line to the throne. This would almost certainly mean the downfall and even execution of Northumberland. He hatched a plan to force Edward to sign a document ignoring Mary and proclaiming his cousin Lady Jane Grey as the rightful Queen instead.

When Edward died soon afterwards, Lady Jane was crowned Queen. But that wasn't enough for Northumberland. He knew there was a great threat of a Catholic uprising, with Mary declared as the leader and rightful Queen. Northumberland's soldiers were sent to arrest Mary. Fearing for her life, at the invitation of the Huddleston family, Mary took refuge at Sawston Hall.

That night, word came that Northumberland's men

knew where she was and were coming to arrest her. With only minutes to spare Mary escaped , some believe, disguised as a milkmaid.

The Protestant soldiers stormed Sawston Hall and set fire to it when they discovered she had escaped. It is said that from Wandlebury Hill Mary looked back at the flames of the burning building and vowed that she would restore Sawston Hall to its former glory when she became Queen.

Northumberland tried to change sides, and threw his hat in the air in Cambridge market place, leading the cheers for Mary. It didn't save him. Mary bravely entered London with her supporters and received a great reception from the people who recognised her as the rightful Queen of England. The cruel tyrant Northumberland was arrested for treason and later executed, as was the teenage Lady Jane.

Mary reigned as a Catholic Queen for only five years, before dying aged only 37. But during her short reign, she kept her word and Sawston Hall was rebuilt from 1557.

But is Mary the grey lady that haunts the building and grounds? A cleaner at the hall has claimed that on one occasion when she was working in the chamber where Mary was supposed to have slept, she felt a presence in the room and saw something make a heavy mark on the bed as though someone had sat down on it.

During the Second World War Sawston Hall was used as a communication centre, linking the fighter bomber base at Duxford aerodrome just three miles away. In 1974 *The Nightcomers,* a Gothic thriller starring Marlon Brando, was filmed at Sawton Hall, I have no idea if Marlon ever saw the ghost of Mary!

Children in my experience love a good ghost story and one I used to recount is the ghosts of the Treasurer's House, next to the magnificent York Minster. In the fifties, an off duty policeman was decorating the basement of the house when he heard a bugle sound and suddenly out of the wall came marching soldiers carrying shields and swords. They passed very close to him. None of the soldiers spoke to him or were aware of him. They all marched in a column towards the opposite wall and disappeared. He told his story to the press afterwards claiming that it was a group of Roman soldiers, as a Roman road originally passed though the house. His claims were ridiculed at first, especially as he described the soldiers as wearing green uniforms, round helmets and carrying round shields, as opposed to the famous Roman red cloaks and square shields. But sometime later archaeologists discovered that the Romans, during their occupation of Britain, often used captured tribes as part of their army, and the remains of soldiers have been found in the York area wearing green uniforms with round helmets and shields.

I decided to take my Year 10 history group on a day visit to York, in 1983 to visit the Victorian museum, the Jorvik centre and of course the Minster. We had a fabulous day in Jorvik and later visited the Treasurer's House. We were greeted by the custodian who told us about the history of the building and gave us a brief tour. My students, who knew the story, wanted to go down into the basement but unfortunately it was closed to the public. However, one or two students, were very persistent, 'Please Mr Reynolds ask him again, we 'd love to see this haunted room.' I did ask again as I was also very interested in seeing it as well. The custodian agreed to take me and four students for a quick tour of the basement. The others left with another member of staff. It was very gloomy down there, damp with mould on the walls. It was also very chilly. Alas we saw no Roman soldiers marching through. However, I did ask the custodian if he had ever witnessed anything strange. He said he had never seen any ghosts but on more than one occasion when he had been working late in the office upstairs he heard bugle sounds and marching footsteps coming from the cellar below. As you could imagine the kids loved that bit and were convinced there was a presence nearby! I thanked him for taking us down to the cellar and asked him quietly on the way out if that was true what he had just said,

'Absolutely true,' he answered. And I believed him which brings me very nicely on to my own ghostly experience at Sawston VC.

One lady, Lily, who for a time was my office cleaner at the college, told me that one early morning before staff and pupils arrived she was busy in the middle school canteen, when she saw a figure standing by the serving hatch which was closed. She said he was wearing a soldier's uniform. When she asked him what he was doing, he didn't look at her but walked forward straight through the wall. She never saw him again. We know that during the war soldiers were trained locally around Sawston and probably used the playground for drills.

On Monday evenings in the Nineties I run a drama group at the college and on this February evening I had to use the Lower school hall as there was a senior youth centre production taking place at the front of the school. I parked on the playground near the tennis courts, which was packed with cars, many people attending the sports and other adult evening classes. After my class finished I took the drama students over to the youth centre to watch the production. It finished quite late and I had to stay till all the children were picked up by their parents. By the time the last parent arrived (there's always one!) everyone else had gone home and the caretaker had turned off the college lights. It was only then that I realised I would have to walk back to pick up my car from the playground which was now in total darkness. I managed to spot a glimmer of light from the roof of my car, about fifty meters away, the only vehicle left on the playground. I walked towards the car and it was then I heard footsteps getting nearer, I was quite relieved at first thinking there was someone else parked nearby and

I wasn't the only one. But I struggled to see another car and all the time the footsteps were getting louder but I couldn't see anyone. I reached my car and the footsteps were very loud, like boots clicking on the concrete. Whoever it was passed straight by my car. I looked up to speak to the person. But there was nobody there. I wasn't scared, it just felt odd.

The footsteps continued as though the person was walking across the playground towards the school building. I started my car up immediately and put the headlights on. Nothing. I drove very slowly down the exit road, still expecting to see a figure walking ahead. No one there. It was and still is an unexplained mystery. I know that I experienced something that night that was very strange that I can't explain to this day. A ghost? Something paranormal? The next day I mentioned this to Lily, I knew she'd be interested. She believed me straight away, 'That was my soldier,' she said, Well, maybe. I never heard ghostly footsteps again.

My grandfather, John Creek, a retired railway driver, built this little cage for the trapped Princess, Jenny Willis, in the school pantomime, guessing Jack in the Beanstalk and I recall driving down to Southend to pick up the costume. Below COUNT ME IN
Chloe, Maria Tatyana

Taken from the play Alys Icognito, Nigel Ashurst marries Kerry Meek Jackson, wearing Sue's original veil. Cheer up Nigel! With Annie Clayton and Tanya Sizer

Chapter Eleven

5 GEN, Biker Boys, 1966 And All that

Oh what fun we had! Rebels definitely without a cause. Here we were in our O level year at the High school, the last few months of our five years coming to an end. Some of us including me, were considering sixth form as I was doing much better academically than in the early years. My friend Richard and I would compete to see who would come top in either history or geography. But of course we were still in 5 GEN the C stream, not good enough for 5A or 5B! Although we were aware of the impending O levels the behaviour and attitude of the members of our form left much to be desired. In negative ways it was though we were fighting back against the elitist system. So what did we do? All sorts.

In PE at last, we were allowed to play football during one lesson on a Friday morning on the field, so that was a huge improvement. Unfortunately, we still couldn't get out of cross country runs. Once a week we checked out at the main gate heading for a route that took us past Long Road and eventually towards the Shelford and Babraham roads. On the way we would stop by the wire fence at The County High school for Girls, now Long Road sixth form college and check out the girls playing hockey, often shouting 'encouraging' remarks, most of which are unprintable. We knew some of their rebel girls as we used to meet up with them at Drummer street after school or hang out in the Guild café. Their teacher was furious, she'd come across and shout at us 'I shall tell your headmaster' while the girls laughed, but not all of them. I think some of the little darlings were horrified by our behaviour. I don't think she ever did tell on us, and there were no cameras in those days and all the fifth year had to traipse across the same route, so she didn't know any names. And our girl mates said they didn't know who we were either.

But that wasn't all, we soon worked out that our teachers rarely monitored us on these runs, often disappearing into the staff room after we'd gone and coming back an hour later waiting to check us in at the main gate. So we discovered a brilliant plan. We would run some of the way but then on the return journey we would catch the 106 bus which took us back down Hills Road, getting off a stop before the school and running the last lap back to the school. We were careful to arrive back in reasonable positions like thirtieth out of ninety, or mid way so the teacher didn't suspect what we were up to. We didn't always take the bus. Sometimes we stopped off near the allotments close to the railway line and had a BBQ! Not quite, we used to take a couple of tins of beans, make a small fire and heat them up. Then spoon them out of the tin. Crazy! Again we were never caught, although on one occasion a hut on the allotments caught fire and burnt down, it was actually reported in the paper. We didn't do it, but it was possible, thinking about it, that we didn't put our fire out properly and sparks had blown onto the wooden hut. Once again we never heard anything so we got away with it.

Nigel, Dave, Roger, my best mate Richard and Tony who was a massive guy, were the main ones in our group. I won't use surnames in order to protect those most certainly guilty. We were no better in the classroom. Our form tutor Mr Murgatroyd,(Name changed) known as Mutt, was a genuinely nice man but a very weak teacher, he had no idea how to teach his subject, which was science. Every Thursday afternoon it was double science and within minutes we soon lost interest as he droned on and on. We'd find all sorts of ways to mess about and disrupt his lesson. During one lesson, Dave had brought an eel to school which he had caught in the river. While Mr Murgatroyd was chalking on the board with his back to us, Dave got the dead eel out of his bag twirled it around his head like a lasso then let it go. Flying though the air, the eel landed on Mr Murgatroyd's shoulder. He looked shocked and no one owned up. I guess as a form we knew we could get away with it with some teachers. Very occasionally we would have what we called a 'love Mutt' day organised by Ali ,when everyone would be co-operative, answer questions and show enthusiasm for the lesson. Mr Murgatroyd would seem rather bemused and couldn't believe his luck. But, of course, it didn't last long, after twenty minutes we'd all had enough of being the goodies and Ali would signal the truce was over and we would revert to our default mode. Poor Mutt, he once stopped a lesson almost in tears and said 'you are driving me to a nervous breakdown.' Now I look back I feel horrified and ashamed at what we did. But we didn't care and Mr Murgatroyd was the fall guy, the one we took it out on after years of existing as third class students trapped, and in some cases despised, in an elitist system.

I don't know what happened to Mr Murgatroyd, but I do recall he also asked about possible careers in form time. He was better as a form tutor. Interestingly, he encouraged me to be a teacher. I also put writer and social worker on the list. Managed the first two but so glad I let the third one go!

Then there was Mrs Smythe, who came for a few weeks as a Maths supply teacher. Very rare to meet a female member of staff . She was nice, a friendly lady with red hair I remember, I think she liked us or at least tolerated us. We worked reasonably well for Mrs Smythe although she didn't escape entirely. One day someone blew up a condom and pinned it to the blackboard before Mrs Smythe arrived for the lesson. I was sitting at the front, Of course she saw the condom straight away, Her face reddened but I could see the start of a smile forming on her lips as she carried on chalking the questions on the board!

Even without the teacher in the classroom we could be quite a raucous bunch, throwing things around and messing about, especially after school, usually in the form room chucking books and wet towels at each other. One day a half eaten banana flew through the air and splattered over the window. No one removed it or cleaned the glass. It stuck to the pane and rotted till it went black. Several months later after I had left the school, I could still see the remains of this rotten banana stuck in the corner of the window that was our form room which overlooked Hills Road.

As most of us were turning sixteen, the summer of '66 became the summer of the motorbike. This was the age of the great British bikes, Norton, Matchless, AJS, Ariel, Royal Enfield and, of course, Triumph. Dad was adamant that I shouldn't have a motorbike, he said he would help me buy a little car but he wouldn't pay a penny towards a bike. So I went out and got a Saturday job and also worked during the holidays and saved up. By the time I was sixteen I had enough money to buy my one and only bike. A Triumph 4 stroke 200cc Tiger Cub. And I loved it. And so did the others in 5 Gen who bought bikes. Suddenly, we were out there travelling around on our machines and mainly going too fast. Richard and I got caught speeding once down Long Road by a Police MG Midget sports car. The officer was very reasonable and let us off with a warning!

Before too long the O levels arrived, we all joked that none of us had revised although I'm sure we had. I was predicted five passes, enough to get me back again in the High school for A levels.

Once the O level exams were over we were allowed to leave. There was no formal assembly, no goodbyes, no leavers' ball or prom night with the County girls, no show, no entertainment. We were told we could leave now and wait for the results. Well, that was never going to be enough for us, On our last official day 5 Gen Biker boys, including me, decided to go out with a bang. Can't remember whose idea it was but we planned to disrupt the whole school assembly by revving up our motorcycles and roaring around the quad and alongside the side of the hall. Several times. It was brilliant, one or two members of staff came out and shouted at us but none of us took any notice. And out we went through the front gate and we were gone.

It was a great summer, an extended holiday and also England won the World Cup. But it all ended in disappointment. I failed to gain the requisite four O levels and was not allowed to join the sixth form. My dad and I visited the Deputy head, George Barlow, in his home. He was a great guy, teaching history, one of the few whose subject I loved. He said he couldn't understand what had happened, I may have been marked down because of my poor handwriting. Nothing's changed! The only option was to return in September and do the fifth year again I managed it for a term, took and passed English Language and then decided to leave and get a job. My old headmaster A W Eagling, gave me a good final report and shook hands with me,believing I might be heading for the Civil Service. But then the Youth Employment Officer secured me a place at the the college of Arts and Technology in Cambridge, to study A level English and History, even though I'd missed the first term. I accepted straight away and had a brilliant time as a student in a completely different environment, a co- educational, comprehensive college. My days at Hills Road were over.

Chapter Twelve

Shell Fish and Mr Chips

Although he wasn't the longest serving member of staff at Sawston VC Roy Petter, Head of History, was undoubtedly our Mr Chips. Roy's teaching career at Sawston spanned three decades until he retired in 1986. He was head of history when I first arrived in 1975 and I couldn't have asked for a better subject leader. Roy was a very unique teacher, a legend at Sawston loved by the staff and thousands of pupils whom he taught. He was a great teacher, combining his considerable knowledge of history with a passion for the subject that inspired so many of his young charges. Roy had a great sense of humour and he was also a very kind man.

There are many things I recall about working alongside Roy. But there are two incidents in particular that I will never forget. Both early mornings when Roy was on bus duty.

Our purpose built history block had four classrooms, a store cupboard and a staffroom. Previous to this, history teachers were dispersed all over the school site. Now we were all together it was so much easier for administration and resources. All the textbooks and work folders could be in one place. The staff room was also a great place for socialising. Most days after school we stayed for coffee and chocolate wafers, we all took turns to bring in biscuits. Staff members often came from other departments to join us. It was a time for humour, relaxation and gossip at the end of the teaching day.

Early one morning I was in the staff room chatting with my history colleague, Kate, before registration when there was a tap on the door. A year 9 pupil Colin, stood in the doorway holding a cardboard box. Colin asked for Mr Petter but I told him that Roy was not available as he was on duty, and could I help?

'Well,' said Colin, 'I went pike fishing in Duxford pits at the weekend and I brought this in for Mr Petter to see. Could you look after it for me until the history lesson period 3?'

I hesitated, thinking the box contained a stinking, decomposing carcass of a pike which I was reluctant to keep in the staff room.

'Is it the remains of a fish?' I asked.

'Oh no, I think it's a shell from the Second World War,' he replied opening the lid of the box, 'I saw it sticking out of the mud, so I dug it up and brought in for everyone to see in history.'

I peered in the box, the shell was about a foot long, covered in grime and rust. I knew that Duxford was a very famous airbase during the Second World War and there were also army contingents based at nearby Sawston Hall, so it was quite likely the shell could have originated from that period. I took the box from Colin and told him I would hand it over to Mr Petter when he arrived. I placed the box on a table in the corner and thought no more of it. I was sorting out some papers when Kate said 'Can you hear that noise?'

'No. What noise?'

'A ticking noise.'

I glanced up at the electric clock on the wall. 'It's the clock, it often makes that noise.'

'No listen, Kelvin, it's coming from over there, where that box is.' And she was right. There was definitely a noise coming from the box. I moved over to the box and opened the lid. The shell was definitely making a clicking noise, and even worse, I touched the metal casing and it was very warm.

'Oh my God, it's a bomb!'

By this time a lot of students were already arriving and filling up the classrooms. In a few minutes the block would reach its capacity of 120 children and four teachers

'We got problems OK, if this thing explodes...'

I carefully closed the lid and picked up the box, 'I'm going to get rid of this, you sound the fire alarm and get everyone outside.'

I carried the box very slowly down the corridor through the double doors and out onto the playground. I headed for a spare piece of land behind the swimming pool which was covered in weeds and brambles. The shell was still ticking. I took it over to the furthest corner and very, very slowly lowered it onto the ground. Then I bolted back to the block as soon as I could! By the time I got back the history block had been evacuated and the Deputy Head had called 999 and the police and Fire brigade were on their way. Classes were reassigned until the emergency was over. However, once the fire service made a cautious inspection of the area they decided to call in the Bomb Disposal group who were located in the army base at Colchester. Roy came over and wondered what was going on.

Two hours later, the squad arrived and the shell was taken away and detonated. Later on that day, the chief officer called the school to inform us that what Colin had found was an incendiary shell, that could have exploded any time. And there was a message for me as well. I was half hoping it was going to be a recommendation for an award. The hero who had saved the school! The message said 'Tell that teacher he was a bloody fool to pick up that box. He could have killed himself and half of the kids in that block.'

Quite right, I didn't get an award and I realised afterwards it was pretty stupid thing to do. It could have exploded any time. From then on I was very careful about what I handled in the classroom especially things that students had brought in for Roy!

One morning I met Roy as he was heading to the playground for bus duty. He told me that we had a new trainee teacher joining the department that day and she would be teaching history for the rest of the term after a suitable period of observation. Roy said he had given the student two of my classes, including the new ancient history course which I had devised. Roy said he had spoken to her on the phone and told her to report to the history staff room, reception would show her the way. But Roy had forgotten that he was on duty so he asked if I would look after her, get her a coffee and make her feel at home until he returned.

'OK, no problem,' I said, 'What's her name?'

'Ah,' said Roy, 'now that's the thing. I can't remember!'

A few minutes later as I was gathering my exercise books for the first lesson there was a knock at the staff room door. I opened it to be met by a very striking girl with long dark hair and a black midi coat that was very fashionable in the seventies.

'Hi,' I'm Marielena,' she said confidently, 'I'm starting here today, I've come to find Mr Petter, he's getting my timetable ready.'

'Hello, yes, he told me. I'm Kelvin,' I said shaking her hand, 'Roy's on bus duty but he will be back soon. Come on in and I'll make you a drink, and by the way call us by our first names.'

Marielena sat down smiling and I opened a packet of chocolate digestives. We talked about her Spanish background, she was most polite and enthusiastic. I already felt that she was going to make a really good teacher and we would get on so well in our department.

'You're going to be with me for a couple of lessons and we will be doing some ancient history, if that's OK.'

'That's fine, I don't really mind, that sounds really interesting.'

'It is. I'm sure you'll be very happy. Any problems we are always here and there's tea and biscuits any time, come in and help yourself whenever you like,' I said, handing her another biscuit.

After a few minutes Roy still hadn't appeared so I left Marielena in the staff room, and went to check if Roy was in his form room. There he was coming down the corridor with a young lady by his side.

'I met Clare coming across the playground,' said Roy. 'This is Kelvin, another history teacher, you will be with him for a couple of classes.'

And I'm like 'Sorry Roy, who is this?'

'This is Clare, our student from Homerton for this term, I told you.'

I shook hands with Clare and said 'Is there another history student from Homerton here today?'

'No,' she said 'I'm the only one.'

'So, Roy, who is the girl sitting in our staff room, then?'

Roy shrugged, 'I don't know what you're talking about.'

Back in the staffroom Marielena was finishing her tea, I sat down at the table beside her.

'Marielena, can I ask you something? Are you from Homerton college?'

'No, why?'

'But you are a trainee teacher?'

She shook her head, looking puzzled. 'I'm not a teacher.'

'If you don't mind me asking, how old are you Marielena?'

'Fourteen,' she said.

'FOURTEEN'!

'Yes, I'm starting here today. Mr Petter is my new Form teacher!'

'But I thought you....' It was a priceless moment!

We let Marielena finish her tea and then Roy took her to her new class. As it happened, she was placed in my history group. Marielena was an outstanding pupil in every way, a delight to teach, she ended up two years later with a top A grade in the subject. But we never forgot that opening day!

Roy was a splendid head of department and we all missed him after he retired. Roy then moved to another village where he worked for a time behind the counter in the local Post Office. He still continued to mark examination papers and support his beloved Cambridge United. When I retired in 2010 I invited him to my retirement party but by this time Roy 's health was declining. But he sent me a wonderful card wishing me well in the future. He did so much to support me in my early years of teaching and it was a joy to work with him. We always felt the history department was unique, and for that we have to thank Roy Petter-our very own Mr Chips.

Chapter Thirteen

Don't cry for me Argentina

If I hadn't become a teacher....

My first paid job at 13 was delivering the Cambridge Evening News, for Barrett's paper shop in Mill Road. My area was around Suez and Hobart Road, six days a week for the princely sum of 40p. We were a good bunch of boys and girls, this was the beginning of the Beatles age. By the time I was 14 I joined the family firm, Reynolds sweets, founded in Newmarket Road by my paternal grandfather James Reynolds. I worked on a Saturday for my Uncle Jim, who kept a shop in Newmarket Road where my dad and his seven siblings were born. I had to be up early as we travelled to Huntingdon market in the land rover, which was quite exciting. My Uncle Jim was always chatting about life and politics on the way and my Auntie Marge would make me a sausage sandwich. I didn't get back home until tea time. On my very first day Uncle Jim left me on the stall by myself for five minutes while he went off to sort something out. I was in charge and very pleased when I got my first customer, a lady who ordered chocolate coconut ice. I had to use a very sharp knife to cut the slab of coconut ice, but unfortunately the knife slipped and cut my finger instead, dripping blood all over the coconut ice. I tried to cut bits off before putting it in a bag. When Uncle Jim returned he found a plaster and a dash of Savlon and I was OK! There were a many other markets and fêtes and fairs we went to, including the Cambridge Midsummer Fair where I worked on the drinks stall along with my cousins Christine and Sandra. But then something else came up.

My friend Paul from High school had got a job during the summer holidays at Jesus Green swimming pool in the little sweet and ice cream kiosk and asked whether I could help. I decided to leave Reynolds sweets and took on Jesus Green six days a week. Oh, what a summer! It was like paradise for Paul and I. We overlooked the lovely pool and served customers poolside and at the rear that opened onto Jesus Green. On hot days it could get very hectic but we loved it and often got to know other teenagers who come up to chat, especially some great girls! One day Ann Rogers and a couple of her friends asked if they could come inside and help us serve, so we let them, which was fine, until the owner's wife arrived to help make the tea and found three girls in bikinis laughing and chatting with us. To be fair, we weren't doing anything and it didn't help when the girls upped and left straight away! Mrs Ladds didn't say anything, and although we thought our poolside days were over, nothing happened and, as a result, I took on a regular Saturday job at the café in Bradwell's Court and then transferred to the yellow caravan in Drummer street, working with Paul for a couple of years. That was a good experience and fun too. The bus station was a focal point for people of all ages. I learnt after some dreadful mistakes, how to make a whippy soft ice cream cone, quite a skill getting the cone just right, keeping the cornet still and not twisting it round. Also it was a good excuse to sample the ice cream every morning to test the machine was ready! After Paul left and moved to Sussex I was now in charge of the caravan. I got a variety of assistants until one week in August 1967 a new girl arrived called Susan. By the end of the week I plucked up courage to ask her out. She said yes, and we're still together today! That one week was the only time I was the boss in our relationship!

    Some of my friends after A level were going into office jobs, earning good money,with good career prospects. Paul had joined the Treasurer's office in Hastings. I wasn't certain that I still wanted to train as a teacher, especially as I now had a regular girlfriend, so I took a job in Accounts and Supplies at the Education department at Shire Hall. It was quite basic stuff really, processing orders for schools. I looked after secondary schools in the county including Sawston Village College. After a while I transferred to the planning department which was more interesting, I could have trained to become a planning officer but when I saw that part of the training involved drawing and sketching and designing new buildings, I knew, being the world's worst drawer, this was not a job for me. I also realised that the job I really wanted to do now was to become a teacher.

And at the last minute in September 1970, just before applications closed, I got a place to study history at Trent Park College of Education in Barnet. Of course becoming a student again meant reduced income, we moved to London and during the holidays I had to take on various jobs, competing with thousands of other students. For a time I worked in a garage at Redbridge serving petrol, it was owned by my parents' neighbour Tony, but it was a long way on the tube every morning from Southgate. The garage has now gone, replaced by Redbridge underground station. There was also traditional student work in the post office, I worked on both parcel delivery vans and street deliveries. That was OK, regular posties were a good bunch. I did make one really bad error, delivered all the cards and letters to the wrong street and had to go and knock on all the doors and ask for them back again! Then I worked in the summer loading lorries at the Merit Toy Factory in Potters Bar, with a couple of other students, hard work but it kept us fit.

But in the summer of 1971 I couldn't find a job anywhere, despite applying for loads of temporary posts. In desperation, I went to the employment office and the guy said he could get me a permanent post as an office worker, but I told him I intended to return to my college course in the autumn. He said 'That's OK. Don't tell them you're leaving.' I got the job telling them I was quitting teaching. So I had to act a lie for a few weeks. I wasn't comfortable with that but it got easier as time went on. It was a company based in Islington, that imported and marketed tins of corned beef, primarily from Brazil and Argentina. I never liked corned beef but the office was a good place. One day an executive came over from Argentina, one of the company's main suppliers and worked alongside us for a few days. We got chatting and shared our interest in football, he was also recruiting one or two staff from England. But I was stunned when at the end of the week he offered me an administrative position on his ranch in Argentina, mainly producing beef cattle. Accommodation would be provided on site, for Sue and I. He showed me brochures and it looked great, he had a lovely family and there were horses to ride on the ranch. It was a large complex and for a short while I was very interested, it really would have been an adventure. But I knew in my heart that teaching was what I really wanted to do. I thanked him but turned down the offer and went back to college. I know that was the right decision but sometimes I wonder what would have happened if I had gone, and ever since I've always supported Argentina in the World Cup, apart from England! And I still don't like Corned Beef.

Top photo : Lads who do lunch

Lower Photo: Jamie Peck and friends planting bulbs in Babraham Road, still blooming today

Chapter Fourteen

Flying Circuses

Once a year in the eighties and nineties something magical happened on the Icknield Rec in Sawston. Children walking to school and adults going to work would stop to view the awesome additions that had appeared literally overnight, For grazing on the rec would be camels, llamas and ponies. Behind them, the giant canvas dome proclaiming that Ray Allen's Circus Galaxy was in town. There may have been others as well. In addition to the animals there would be acrobats, jugglers, clowns and trapeze artists on the high wire. One of the owner's children, I will call her Sky, would spend a few days at the college while the circus was in town. It must have been very difficult for any child spending only a few days in one area and one school before moving on somewhere else but Sky was a very pleasant and able pupil. She came to us on a couple of occasions but it was obvious that circus was her first love. I did a story about the circus and Sky invited me to visit her home and working area to meet the other performers and show me around. The caravans were quite small where they lived, and performers would also help to erect the tent and look after the animals in between performances. It was a tough life, and a real team effort. Everyone I spoke to made me feel welcome. My children and I went to see the circus on a couple of occasions and watched as Sky was put in a box and apparently cut in half! Later she showed me how it was done but my lips are sealed!

It was great entertainment, a small circus compared with the giant rings of Billy Smart, but it was still a circus, giving new acts a chance to perform and our village an opportunity to experience the thrill of the circus on our doorstep. Sky was immensely proud of her family and her part in the circus.

But we too had our own circus acts at the college on a permanent basis. Louise Baxter, when she was only thirteen was probably the best young contortionist in the country. Louise or to use her stage name, the Amazing Louise, was in my year group and took part in occasional drama sketches and the video *Wild Strawberries*, although her parts were limited, for most weekends and evenings Louise was working as a contortionist in many exciting shows, including television, the theatre and circuses. Her act truly was amazing, I have never seen any one perform like Louise. Her own classmates called her Bendy Baxter and looked on in awe as she twisted her body into the most incredible positions. One occasion my drama group performed as part of a radio charity day at Addenbrooke's hospital in Cambridge. Louise was with me. Patients came down to watch us perform in the foyer. However there was one patient who was not allowed out of bed in the hospital, she was upset that she missed our show. I was asked if we could go up to the ward and perform for her, which we did, and not surprisingly Louise stole the moment! Also on that day, I was asked to look after a young TV star from a stage school who acted in a ITV comedy programme, she was there with two others to support the charity. Kelly met my drama students for a time and during a break I got her a drink and we sat down and had a chat before she resumed her promotion work.

Kelly was about fourteen then, I recall her being very confident and very pleasant, wearing make up but she was a TV star. And still is. Kelly Bright went on to act in several programmes until landing a major role as Linda in EastEnders where she can still watch her most nights behind the bar in the Vic on the BBC.

Returning to Louise, she also appeared in many talent shows on TV and stage including BBC Superstore, and also won several medals and awards including a £1000 holiday in Germany at the South coast Star awards Her unique talent also meant that she was often asked to appear in historical cabaret such as Tudor fayres and feasts. She was often featured in local television and many magazines. Louise was also in demand for circus performances, including a summer season in Cornwall with Jay Miller Circus and Paulo's circus in Cambridge. It was a great honour for Louise to be chosen to appear in a Royal Gala evening, at the Gordon Craig theatre Stevenage, performing before HRH Prince Edward, with Nigel Hawthorne, Dame Judy Dench and principals from the Royal Ballet.

Louise was always busy but so modest, a lovely girl always smiling, enjoying her life through her own amazing talent. And often she would appear in my office during the week and request permission to be absent on Friday afternoon as she was involved in a weekend project in another part of the country and had to arrive in time for rehearsals and stage and studio checks. I never said no, her parents too were very supportive. I knew this was her life and her dream for the future, I did all I could to encourage her. Although on one occasion the Deputy head was not happy with me for allowing her absence on a regular basis but I persuaded him to let her have the time off. She always managed make up the work.

Louise left school and moved away to pursue a career in showbiz, always her dream, but sadly it was not to be. By a remarkable coincidence we were shopping in Bedford one day and I met Louise in the town centre. She was no longer a contortionist, the years of contorting her body into incredible shapes had taken a toll on her growth and the development of her bones and muscles, and there was high risk that to continue with the act could lead to permanent disability. But she left us with great memories and an amazing impression on all who witnessed her remarkable act.

Here are some comments

'An amazing performance,with immaculate stage props, beautifully presented.' Peter Hepple, Stage and TV Today.
'You have a charming personality,' Dame Judy Dench
'I am honoured to have you on my show and dedicate my next song to you.' Johnny Logan, twice Eurovision contest winner for Ireland 'I liked your act very much. You are very, very good.' HRH Prince Edward.

We must also say at Sawston we had our own juggler and circus skills teacher in Eddie Konig, who did many workshops and still does for the Cambridge Commnuity groups now he has retired, both in the UK and abroad.

Chapter 15

Mad Dogs and History teachers go out in the morning sun

After a reasonable first teaching practice at the Albany secondary school in Enfield, my second was at a junior school, Holly Park, Barnet. It was a challenge to teach a class of 32 nine year olds,

On my first day at break time as I was having a coffee, the Head, Mrs Maxwell, came into the staffroom and announced 'which gentlemen is going to give up their chair for me?' She looked directly at me so I mumbled something and got up. To me all the chairs seemed exactly the same but I was sitting in her special chair. She observed one of my lessons right at the end of the day when all the kids in my class were sitting on the floor and I was asking questions about the topic we had studied. She told me afterwards it was like a grammar school lesson, needless to say it wasn't my best experience. Primary school teachers have to teach everything, I managed the Maths and English, I recall designing work cards, but I knew this wasn't right for me. I preferred the subject orientated Secondary school. But there was one incident at Holly Park that I shall never forget.

Every morning I walked to school from our flat in Southgate across the park in Friern Barnet to reach the school. It was a fine day in early spring. Suddenly I was aware of a large dog, barking furiously and hurtling towards me. The dog pinned me up against a tree, he didn't bite but his teeth were very close to my face. I managed to get my briefcase between us as some kind of protection. The dog reacted to the slightest movement, snarling and threatening to bite. There was no one else around, no owner coming to rescue me. So I had to stay there trapped against the tree for I don't know how long, not daring to move. Then I had a brainwave. I remember my dad telling me that when he travelled as an agricultural rep to various farms, if he was ever met by a hostile dog, he would always carry a few dog biscuits which he would throw on the ground and this usually quietened them down. I didn't have any dog biscuits but I did have something that might work. My packed lunch, egg sandwiches made by Sue. Very, very carefully I flicked the metal clip on my brief case and slowly delved inside. I felt the packet of sandwiches. The dog snapped at my briefcase. I pulled out the sandwiches and managed to throw one down on the ground. The dog's behaviour changed immediately, he let me go and started woofing down the sandwich. I crept around the tree and threw more bread a little bit further away. Amazingly, this worked and after a couple of minutes I was getting further away. Eventually I threw all that was left of my packed lunch at various points near to the dog which kept him occupied. When I felt safe enough I bolted towards the exit, so relieved to get away. On reaching the school, late of course, I reported what had happened. I didn't want anyone else to get trapped, especially a child. The police came and searched the park. They never did find the dog. They said it could have been a guard dog that escaped from a house.

In some ways it was the best egg sandwich I have ever had, and I never walked through that park again! Thanks Dad.

My final teaching practice was at Heathcote, a secondary school in Stevenage. This lasted a few months, teaching mainly history. It was a good school overall. Whenever a member of staff appeared in the doorway all the class would stand up and wait till they were told to sit down. On my birthday Mum had sent in a birthday request for me to the Jimmy Young show on

BBC Radio 2 and it was read out live on air by his special guest that day, Hollywood legend Cary Grant. Stevenage was mentioned but pronounced 'Stefanige' by Cary! And the next day there was another surprise. I was called in by the Head, Mr Lewis, who came to watch me teach a lesson a few days earlier. He offered me a job saying I think you would be good for the school and the school would be good for you. By coincidence I had also applied and got an interview at the Ailwyn school, part of the Abbey College in Ramsey.

It was a good place to be, I liked the Stevenage school and settling in wouldn't have been hard as I had spent so many weeks teaching there already. But equally, I was impressed with the buildings and atmosphere of Ramsey, a much more rural environment than the concrete blocks of Stevenage. Also Ailwyn school hinted they would probably be able to provide a staff cottage in the village if I accepted the job. In the end, I turned down both jobs with some reluctance. The reason was that I had completed the Teacher's Certificate exam and I had gained Part One of the B. Ed. qualification. I could postpone studying for part two of the B.Ed degree for up to five years and carry on teaching, at either of the schools who had offered me jobs. But my tutor pointed out that if I stayed one more year I would have a degree and that would mean starting at a higher salary in just twelve months. After all, he said, if you've got two offers now think how many you will get next year when you have a degree. How wrong he was!

Despite applying for numerous history posts in the spring of 1975 I was very disappointed not to get any offers. St Bede's, Coleridge, Bassingbourn, Greneway Middle school, Royston, all interviews but no job at the end of it. And even Sawston VC! I was interviewed and turned down as the history post was offered to David Dobson, a Cambridge graduate. He was also a keen sportsman with a talent for music and drama. I somehow knew I wasn't going to get that one. I was very disappointed as SVC seemed such a lovely school, and made a great impression on me. By Easter I hadn't found a job for September, and the County Council suggested I might want to go on the supply list which would offer valuable experience and a salary. I thought in the circumstances it was better than nothing, And then it happened. My mum took a call from Mr Marven, the Warden at Sawston, (I wasn't on the phone and there were no mobiles then) asking if I could come back for a second interview as another job was available if I wanted it. I made an appointment straight away for the next day. It wasn't for the original history post, but a general subjects post covering some history, geography, PE and social economics, which I knew little about but I was very willing to learn! A few weeks later I spent a day visiting the school, in the company of Roy Petter, my new head of History.

It was a very good day. As I drove home I knew that I would be going back in September, ready to start my career as a professional teacher-at last!

When I was on supply around 2017, this young lady in Year Seven made me a pyramid out of sugar cubes! I can't recall her name to credit her for this, if anyone knows her do let me know. She left a year or two ago.

Chapter Sixteen

Being Helen Barton

I have met and worked with some amazing students in my time at Sawston, but none quite compares with the one and only Helen Barton, who entered the school into my year 7 year group in 1988.

When I turned forty in 1990 I woke up to find balloons and ribbons tied to the lamppost outside my house in Princess Drive, not from the neighbours and not from my family. This turned out to be Helen and her friend Laura Myers who had got up early and decided to add to my celebrations ! A lovely thing to do, and this was just the start!

Helen loved music and was always willing to help on my shows and my video productions, usually operating sound and music and one occasion we filmed a sequence from Blue Twilight in a room in her house. She was also there to provide music for the party sequence which took place in Louise Moore's house in Trumpington, around 9.00 in the morning. Always reliable and a joy to work with. So far so good. Then in year nine, during activities week, Derek Cupit planned a production of the Pirates of Penzance for those students not on residential trips. We started rehearsing on the Monday morning, ready to perform the musical live three days later in front of parents. Quite a challenge, as many of the students who didn't go away were not into drama. But Derek was so good at motivating people and it was quite fun to be involved. I was given the part of the police sergeant, with one song to perform, rehearsals went quite well but on the night it was a disaster. First verse was fine, second verse I completely dried up halfway through. My mind went blank. From behind a piece of scenery on stage Helen was shouting the words and in front of me

Janet McLeod was conducting and she did a fantastic job accompanying me. How I got to the end of the song I don't know. But it was great fun and all credit to the cast and to Derek for a not to be forgotten performance. Afterwards I met Alan Cleveland, who belonged to the Shelford Light opera group, and I asked him what he thought. He told me 'I've seen many productions of the Pirates of Penzance over the years but never seen one quite like that!'

One morning after break Helen appeared in my yr 9 history class looking at a magazine. She said she was entering a competition which she had started during break time and could she carry on for a few minutes to finish. I was like 'No, you'll have to finish it later,' but I could see Helen was not giving up. In the end I asked what the competition was about. Apparently, she had to make up a name for a thrilling new ride to be opened in the summer at Alton Towers. The winner would be invited along for the special opening. 'You can have five minutes and that's it,' I said. She put the magazine away and carried on with the lesson. I thought that was the end of it.

A few weeks later Helen came to class. 'Guess what? You know that Alton towers competition I entered in your lesson, I won!' And it was true. The theme park had chosen Helen's entry as the name for the new ride. Helen was invited up to Alton Towers for the official opening and shared the first ride with celebrity Philip Schofield. Despite his recent troubles, Philip was quite famous in the nineties apart from television presenting, he also played the lead in Joseph and the Amazing Technicolour Dreamcoat at the Palladium, I organised a school trip one Saturday to see the matinee performance.

The ride is no longer in operation but it was quite an honour for Helen, maybe she wouldn't have come up with that name if it hadn't been for that history lesson. (Helen doesn't remember the name of the ride).

During activities week the school also organised a day

trip to the water park Tubes near Dartford tunnel, I think it was called Fantaseas. I was quite surprised how high the tubes were, twisting in different directions until you landed in a splash pool at the end. I was supervising students at the top of one of the tubes which had flashing disco lights inside. It looked good fun and encouraged by the students I thought I might have a go. BIG MISTAKE. Once I sat on the platform, I realised it was quite dark and I didn't want to do it as I'm a bit claustrophobic. Unfortunately, Helen was right behind me and before I could change my mind she gave me a push and I found myself sliding down quite fast. I recall it was hot and stuffy then it went dark and I got stuck on a bend. I panicked, my heart was racing and it took all my efforts to push myself forward again. It was such a relief to literally find light at the end of the tunnel as I plunged into the splash pool. Helen arrived right behind me seconds later. I stood up pretending to be amused and swung my arm back 'Don't you ever do that again,' I gasped. Unfortunately my hand caught Helen in the face. And knocked her new brace out of her mouth. The brace landed in a drainage channel at the side of the pool, we chased it but I couldn't get hold of it. I watched in horror as it disappeared down a drain at the end. I was very apologetic, especially when Helen told me it had only been fixed at the dentist a week before! I visited her home and apologised to Helen's mum, Apparently, I don't remember this, I took her box of maltesers. Helen was able to get another brace made and we joked about it at school but I never went into a a tube again!

    After Helen left school she went to study A levels at Hills,Road and we kept in contact, occasionally she popped round for coffee and a chat. I was thrilled when she invited Sue and I to her 18th birthday party held at the Red Lion, Whittlesford. Later University followed. But by this time, Helen was a great fan of rock star Bryan Adams and would regularly go to his concerts, meeting up with a few other fans. I find it incredible that Helen has seen Bryan perform 166 times! including many trips abroad. He recognises her in the audience She has even been invited up on stage to sing with him. Amazing! And very recently when Bryan appeared on the One Show they showed a clip from one his concerts and there in the front row was Helen!

She still had time to fit in concerts by other pop stars. One of her other favourites is James Blunt. I love his music too so in 2012 James appeared at the Corn Exchange in Cambridge I got myself a ticket. Helen with her friends and mum, Peggy, arrived early and joined the queue so that they would be able to get a place at the front of the stage. It was standing only. I couldn't get there early as I was teaching a drama class at Stapleford Primary after school. Helen very kindly kept me a place with her group and I arrived just before the doors opened. We were right at the front, I got to meet Helen's mum again and her friends, it was brilliant, I still play his music.

Helen still tours Europe and even the USA to see Bryan Adams. Shenow commissioning editor for Cambridge University Press and so often visits other countries to set up a stand and promote the company's books. It's a bonus if one her favourite groups is appearing nearby. In 2018 she appeared as a a guest on my show at Radio Addenbrooke's in Cambridge. There was torrential rain that day and I wanted to cancel as she was cycling from work that afternoon, but Helen insisted she would be there, so she arrived dripping in the foyer and it was lovely to see her again. In between the music of Bryan Adams and James Blunt we reminisced about our times together at Sawston. In quieter moments. I see pictures of Helen on facebook relaxing at home with her lovely cats and usually with a glass of wine in her hand, something else we have in common! I am very proud of Helen's achievements. She is a fantastic person, full of fun. Thank you Helen, for all the wonderful memories and the adventures we had together at Sawston and beyond. I shall never forget you.

Oh yes Principal, do pop in and have a look at my Year 8s working hard

Three years later, same class in year 11 introduce new school uniform for SVC! Kim, Hayley Bade, Nicola, Jo, Jamie Stacey and the rebel Mr Cragg among others

Chapter Seventeen

If music be the food of love play on..

My first introduction to David Adams was at the Lower school assemblies, he was the pianist who led the hymns in 1975. I got to know him as one of the great characters of SVC, a very talented musician and Head of music, David was one of the speakers at John Marven's funeral. His wife Tricia worked in the library.

Lucy Barlow succeeded David, and like him, always supported the Youth Centre productions once or twice a year. Lucy helped with the production of Last Flower On Earth, as did Dave. Later Janet McLeod became head of Music. The music at Sawston was always of the highest standard from the choirs and the orchestra. St Mary's Carol concert always a highlight plus the annual concert at West Road.

Following Derek Cupit as Youth Centre Director, was Mark Long. I taught Mark originally in my first year at College, in year nine history. He used to do impersonations then. Mark is a brilliant inspiration and has directed all major youth centre productions since, shows of the highest quality. He has done so much for the community of Sawston supported, by many others, choreographers, stage workers and, of course, musicians. Mark developed concerts also for both year 7s and year 8s with the help of the exceptional Gareth Furbank. None of us who were privileged to witness it could ever forget Richard Furbank's performance in *Jesus Christ Superstar,* a performance that would have graced any professional stage. And then there was Grace Furbank, unique and versatile, so enjoyed working with her

Mark and Gerry first decided to launch a Sawston pop idol show over twenty years ago, we had the auditions then first round public heats before the final, usually held in the spring term. It was an honour for me to be asked as one of the judges, we would all comment on each performance and we tried to be as positive as we could for each act. Before the final there was always a few weeks of rehearsals to prepare. Loved doing Pop Idol, saw some brilliant acts. Amy Fallon, a year seven pupil, was our youngest ever winner singing *I wish I knew you before.* Cameron Carr, what a singer! he could tackle any style and he went on to perform and tour with the the King's singers His sister Emmeline, also very talented entered most years, I remember *These boots are made for walking* and *Downtown* which she performed brilliantly.

Alice Boagey who won the competition was also a judge on one occasion. But it wasn't just about winners, it was fabulous to see so many pupils brave enough to audition and also to get such a great support from a local audience.

And there was Suzie Curran, I have included a piece on Suzie and her amazing talented family later on.

Alison Nicholls, the one and only harpist I have ever known. Alison plays so beautifully, her talent was evident even as a young student at the college. And this amazing talent has taken her to so many prestigious concerts and international fame. She won a place at the world famous Juilliard school in New York and is regarded as one of the finest players of her generation. I believe she still plays and gives private lessons today. It was a joy after she left school that she returned to Sawston on occasions to play a piece for us.

ALISON NICHOLLS

Ruth Sanderson (Catton) another gifted student whom I met covering a Maths lesson in yr 11. Ruth, I believe, used to sing in the choir but she also composed and wrote her own songs, music that I think is so unique. I invited Ruth to perform at the School fête one year. She sat at the piano and played several songs, all of which she had written herself. What a talent she was. She made me a cassette tape back in the nineties (no CDs then) with all her songs on, including one that we wrote together, called *Wild Card*. Well, I did the lyrics which were not as good as Ruth's! Today Ruth says her songs are ramblings and teenage angst. Not true. I think her music is beautiful and really connects. I love listening to Ruth's own unique style and I wish we had the opportunity in 1990s for Ruth to upload her songs on platforms like Youtube and Sound cloud. I'm hoping we might be able to find a way to do this in the future.

I have included an extract of the lyrics from one of the songs but you really have to listen to the song to appreciate Ruth's talent.

> Bent old cards
> Ruin the game
> Bunsen burner boiling tube
> Purple flame
> Misconstrued
> Passing Phase time will heal
> Force converge
> Silently yield
> Any time you want you can use my shampoo.....
> just call me tonight and I will bring it round to

you.

Ellie Dixon was only at the school for one year but she did the most beautiful work of the highest standard. I taught her for geography. She was a very small girl in year 7, but had a wicked sense of humour. She excelled in Maths and science. In my very last parents' evening, Ellie Dixon was the last appointment, it was lovely to finish talking about her fantastic work. Now you're probably wondering what's this go to do with music? Ellie left Sawston in year 7 and I never saw her again until she was a sixth former. I was very surprised to meet her at Strawberry Fair singing and playing guitar with her friend for local radio. I had no idea she was into music, She carried on playing at Warwick University and was becoming quite established by the time she graduated. Her music went from strength to strength, composing her own songs, often very quirky, she became one of the BBC new musicians of the year, and has been featured on Mollie King's show on BBC Radio 2. I was lucky enough to host Ellie on my radio show at Radio Addenbrooke's a few years ago where she played live. Typical of Ellie, she came on the bus carrying her guitar. Since then Ellie has played the Junction in Cambridge, signed for Decca Records and completed a European tour as a headline act. This year she played at Glastonbury. You can find Ellie on her website and listen to some of her music.

ELLIE DIXON

I can't use Shakespeare's, quote again but to all these wonderful people I've written about above, I salute you. *You are simply the best THANK YOU FOR THE MUSIC*

So here I am, someone who can't play or read a note of music, working with musical theatre and talent shows. I loved every minute and I'm still in awe of the wonderful teachers and the amazing talented kids. But at least I could do one thing. I could do a reasonable rendition of *Wonderwall* or another Oasis hit during the school Revues, as long as Adrian Lockwood accompanied me on the guitar, I think once we also played with a boy band with Brian Higgins' son on guitar. Apologies to hundreds of classes that have had to put up with me humming or singing in lessons, I'm just the same at home.

*Although *Leanne Carlin* was always going on about my Oasis numbers! I think she liked them really

Chapter Eighteen

Moscow - Behind the Iron Curtain

In 1978 I was lucky to be part of one of the most amazing school trips I have ever been on, the first time that students and staff from Sawston Village College visited Moscow. That was history in itself. We were very excited, and a little apprehensive, as we were going behind the iron curtain It was also a very interesting time of history. The Russians were increasing tourist opportunities as they prepared to host the Olympic Games in 1980. My colleague, David Dobson, organised the trip, with Soviet tourist agency Intourist. We were to fly with Aeroflot from Heathrow direct to Moscow and would be staying in a hotel for a week during the October half term.

The local news took a photo of our group as we boarded our coach on the way to Heathrow, a party of about 25 students and four staff. At that time I hated flying, my limited experience confined to holiday trips to Spain. My fear of flying was such that I was once given a tranquilliser at Gatwick airport by a nurse before boarding a flight to Majorca, as I didn't think I was going to make it and feared having a panic attack mid-air. The tranquilliser worked. From then onwards, if ever I was about to fly I would visit the GP beforehand and obtain prescribed tablets that I would have to take before the flight, with enough left for the return journey.

I was getting quite anxious about the impending trip to Moscow and considered pulling out at one stage but then I felt I could not withdraw from such an exciting trip, especially as a history teacher, the opportunity may never come again.

At Heathrow, in the departure lounge, the students had some time to themselves before we arranged to regroup for boarding. I went off to look at the shops and find a time to take my pill. I met some of our group and asked them if they had seen Mr Dobson. Nobody had, which I thought was odd. Eventually, I found Dave with his wife, Joyce, sitting in a corner. That's when he told me. He had never flown before and was absolutely petrified! He didn't think he would make the flight. At first I didn't know what to do because Dave had all the documents and details as party leader, we just had to get him on that flight. And that's when I had a brilliant idea, something you should never do of course, I offered him one of my tranquillizers, which he took. I knew I would have enough for myself and for the return journey. I told him not to worry and sit quietly and let the tranquilliser work, I would get all the students together with the help of Audrey, our other female member of staff. Audrey was a lovely lady, ideal to have as a staff member for a school trip. But I couldn't find her either until someone told me she was in the bar drinking a stiff whisky as she was frightened of flying! Fortunately, this worked! Audrey returned and then it was time to board the plane. The students were very excited, it was a massive plane, Aeroflot's Il -62, with double engines at the rear, very similar design to our VC -10s.

I sat next to Daphne Clark and Dawn Hughes, original members of my form and across the aisle was David, looking very pale. As the plane taxied, Daphne, who had never flown before, said 'It's just like being on a bus!' The engines roared and we took off. I glanced across at Dave, his eyes were closed and he was gripping the arms of his seat as the plane banked steeply over London before heading East towards Moscow, actually only four hours flying time. Once in the air, David was still gripping the seat, wishing away every minute. I sympathised with his situation, I had been there several times. I had a quick check on our students, they were all fine. I sat down again, soon we were ordering our meals, I chose a curry, it was lovely. As we approached

Moscow the sun was going down and I recall a fabulous purple and gold autumn sky. By this time David was feeling a bit better which was a relief. It was only as we strapped ourselves in for landing that it suddenly occurred to me I hadn't taken my own tranquilliser! For the first time in years I had flown without any anxiety issues, and without any pills to calm me down. Looking back I think taking over from Dave temporarily took my mind off my own fears as I had to take responsibility and focus on the welfare of the students. In fact that was a major turning point. I love flying now, I have never had any problems since or felt the need to take tranquillisers. And so four hours later on a Saturday evening we arrived at Moscow's Sheretyevo Airport. Our adventure had begun!

The Hotel Berlin where we stayed was situated in the heart of the city, one of Moscow's oldest hotels. It had old style elegance about it and I was impressed with the accommodation compared with some of the hotels we had stayed in on previous school trips to France. The staff were friendly although not many could speak English. Food was good although some of the students didn't take to the meatballs and vegetables, a popular dish in the seventies. And there was always ice cream. The Russians love ice cream and even in the depths of the Russian winter families buy ice cream.

We had our own guide, Alexei, a friendly and helpful young man who spoke very good English. He would accompany us on every trip. Alexei was a prominent member of the young Communist group and he showed us pictures of himself with high ranking politicians including General Secretary Brezhnev, at various conferences. I think it's fair to say Alexei's job was to keep an eye on us and to ensure we kept to the official plan on any excursion. We did some lovely trips, we had a choice between the Moscow State Circus and The Bolshoi Ballet, which was next to our hotel. I would have loved to have seen the ballet, especially as

Tchaikovsky is my favourite composer but the kids chose the circus, where we enjoyed front row seats and I have to say it was brilliant. On coach tours we also saw the University buildings and preparations taking place for the Olympics. We visited the Lenin Mausoleum, it was very strange and somewhat eerie to see Lenin's embalmed body lying on a bed. I believe it closed a few years ago.

But for me the best visit was to a language school in Moscow. It was an all girls school and some of the older students did presentations about Russian history and their involvement in the Second World War. The students spoke fluent English, I was very impressed with their knowledge and the pride they showed for the soldiers of the motherland who sacrificed so much in the fight against Hitler. Afterwards, David decided that we would do something for them. He played the piano and we sang the Beatles song *Yesterday*, and the Russian girls joined in. It was a lovely moment and I think his idea did so much to bring our two groups closer together. Sadly, no mobiles then to record the scene.

Towards the end of trip we we were taken to an ice hockey match, and it was interesting that there was little audience participation, apart from polite applause, where as our students were cheering and whooping for the home side, which got us curious looks from the rest of the audience!

Every morning we would see the people from our hotel windows queuing outside the GUM store, one of the biggest in Moscow, to buy food and other provisions. On the streets there was always a police presence. One of our students, Mark, asked if he could take a picture of a policeman in the street but it became very clear from his hostile stare and the way he pointed to his black and white baton swinging from his belt this wasn't going to happen. I nodded and smiled and we moved away quickly!

It was also a very strange experience to be in a country

where apart from the guide and some hotel staff, hardly anyone spoke English, not what we had been used to in France and Spain.

One morning as we waited to cross a main road the traffic was held up as a line of black limousines with police outriders drove past. The windows were blacked out but we were told that Leonid Brezhnev himself was inside. But there was one place we had to see. The Kremlin and Red Square. Just a short walk from our hotel and close to the River, its impressive red walls and turrets line Red Square on one side and overlook the River to the south. Behind these walls lie a myriad of buildings such as churches, palaces, museums and even gardens. The beautiful St Basil's cathedral is the highlight, bordering one side of Red Square. I bought a miniature version as a present for my mother which I have now, also lots of the students purchased the Russian dolls painted and made of wood, which open up to a smaller one inside, like eggs, and this continues until you reach a tiny doll at the end. Fascinating stuff. On our last evening, Julie, a sixth form student previously at Sawston, asked whether she could go to Red Square and take a few final pictures, and would I go with her for a few minutes. Dusk was falling but the lights were coming on in the Kremlin and Red Square. Julie took her pictures and as we walked across the Square it started to snow. It was a very surreal and beautiful moment. We were total strangers alone, right in the heart of one of the famous cities in the world, a country that was perceived as the enemy behind the iron curtain. I shall never forget that last night with Julie

in Red Square. The next day we departed for the airport. I think Dave took another tranquilliser, but he was much better on the return flight. I decided I didn't need one. It had been an incredible experience, quite an emotional one for us all. We had seen life behind the Iron curtain and had some amazing experiences during our short visit. We felt like pioneers and over the next few years more and more schools would visit the country.

Chapter Nineteen

The Great Fire of Sawston VC.

September 2012.

    It was only the second day of term, and I was meeting for the first time a new Yr 7 class for Citizenship. It was the last period of the day and I had only just started with the course introduction and the names of the students when the fire alarm went off. Normally, we have regular fire practices, but not usually this early in the term. It was quite annoying as I was just settling the class down. I assured the class it was just a drill and we would be back in fifteen minutes. Following regulations all students had to leave their coats and bags in the classroom and make their way to the Assembly points on the field. I turned out the lights and joined my class in the access road outside our block that led to the field. It was then that a little girl grabbed my sleeve and said 'Mr Reynolds LOOK!' A dense plume of smoke rose into the sky above the main Edinburgh wing, I realised then it was no drill but something potentially serious.

    We reached the playing field and I lined up the class to take the register. By now I could see the buildings on fire. The flames shooting in the air were so hot our faces burned as though we were standing next to a bonfire. In fact we were about 100 meters away,. There was a moment of shock from everyone when we saw and felt the extent of the fire. Some of the younger pupils became frightened and upset, and at this stage we didn't know if any students or staff were trapped in the classrooms. The air was filled with smoke and burning debris and we could hear the screaming sirens getting closer to the school.

    Our Principal was out at a meeting at another school

and didn't know of the unfolding drama at SVC, but deputy Principal Jonathan Russell now the actual principal, did a fantastic job organising staff and children in a very calm and efficient manner. I was very impressed. It's what leadership's all about in times of crisis The fire crews battled to keep the fire from spreading to the main hall. We were still trapped on the field in our teaching groups and were not allowed to go anywhere near the buildings. A complete register check showed that every member of staff and all students were safe which was the top priority By now several worried parents had gathered at the front of the school, alarmed about the fire and their children inside. My son, David, who was at work had seen a breaking news report online and phoned Sue and said did she know Sawston VC was on fire? She didn't.

The flames continued to burn and it was late afternoon before some of the classrooms well away from the fire were declared safe for the children to collect their belongings. It was getting on for six before we were all able to depart. I saw briefly the extent of the damage. The whole wing of the Fountain court had been completely destroyed including the village library, the famous walnut meeting room and the staff room. But the fire fighters had managed to stop the fire spreading into the roof of the main assembly hall. That evening the fire was featured on local television.

The next day the school was closed but Sue and I went to look at the damage, the smell of burning still in the air. It was hard to take in the destruction of such a large part of the school and it would take many months, even years before it was returned to its former glory. As this part of the school was a grade 2 listed building, special materials had to be used in the rebuilding, such as plaster in the walls and roof. Temporary classrooms were brought on site, although most of the damage was done to other rooms rather than classrooms. Corridors were boarded up and a one way system put in operation.

We could only use the Lower school hall for assemblies while repairs were made to the ceiling and walls of the main hall. Sadly too, with the Fountain Court also out of bounds, the Leavers' Ball could not be held on site and was transferred for a time to Duxford aerodrome. But eventually all repairs were completed and the wing rebuilt, which now contains the main office and reception. And the Leavers' ball has returned to the college.

There was building work taking place in that wing before the fire broke out and it is believed that it was caused accidentally by a hot air gun being used for alterations to windows, according to a report from Heart Radio. The flames quickly took hold in the roof and spread through the rest of the building. It is interesting to observe that our fire in 2012 had certain elements in common with the Great Fire of London in 1666. Both started on a warm day in September with dry conditions and a moderate breeze that helped fan the flames. Fortunately, our fire was contained very swiftly by the fire services and there were no casualties or mass destruction of buildings as witnessed in London.

It was lovely to receive a message the next day from Heidi Morgan,(now Crane) one of our teaching Assistants at SVC at the time. Heidi's daughter, Carmen, was in my class that day and she was previously a member of my drama group at Stapleford primary school. Heidi thanked me for keeping Carmen and all the other pupils safe in my care during what was a very frightening experience for the new Year sevens on only their second day.

From then onwards I realised how quickly a small fire can spread, causing massive damage and a threat to life. In any place of work or school I can't emphasise enough the importance of regular fire drills. We can replace burnt out buildings, we can't replace people.

While many people remember the fire of 2012, only a few will remember an earlier fire in 1974. On my first official visit to Sawston Village College after my appointment in April 1975, I was taken to see my new classroom in the language block where I would be having a form in September. It was quite a shock to find all the rooms had no windows and the walls were black and stained with smoke, all the furniture gone. A few months earlier a kiln in the art room on the second floor caught fire during the night and most of the block was destroyed. Fortunately, the building could be repaired and I was assured by September it would be ready. And so it was, Room 26 on the ground floor contained brand new desks, fresh paint work and a bank of shiny lockers, ready for my first classroom and my first form 1R

WALKING WITH WOLVES 2000

Holly, one of several cats in my life who brought me so much joy. Loved them all

Chapter Twenty

Queen Bees on Stage

Derek Cupit. The legend. What a character. Senior Tutor at SVC for many years but best known for his fabulous youth centre musical productions, running from the late sixties till the eighties. I first came across Derek when Gerry Holloway recruited a few of the male staff to play dainty little fairies in the middle of the school pantomime in 1975. Derek did the choreography, we were dressed in ridiculous costumes, shorts and nighties, it was really funny but Derek's stern message was

'Don't play for laughs, play it for real keep it serious, that's where the laughs will come.'

Later on I became stage manager for a couple of Dave Dobson's productions, and in early 1981 co- produced my first and only pantomime 'Jack in the Beanstalk' with Brian Higgins. From then on I started a drama group with younger pupils at lunchtime, but I wanted to focus not on musicals but improvised work based on the ideas and inspiration of Anna Scher, who formed a wonderful drama group in North London for local children. It was then I decided I wanted to write scripts for my group and transfer to an evening class, as lunchtime could be quite tight for time. This meant I needed permission from Derek as Senior Youth Tutor responsible for evening classes and at first he wasn't that happy. I think he was worried that my group of 11-14 yrs might in some way interfere with his group. But he soon realised that in our group we focused on issue based dramas for teenagers and was in no way in opposition to the youth centre. In fact, Derek became a very good supporter of my productions, his advice was invaluable but I think we won his respect with our work. We called ourselves The Elite, pretentious I know, and we used to meet every Monday evening. It was open to all students from 11-14, for a small fee, sometimes there could be up to thirty present. It was fun and the group continued for many years. And from this group I cast the plays that we performed, first in assemblies, then by 1990 moving on to the Sawston and Cambridge Drama Festivals, performing at the Mumford theatre. And what a group it was!

Alys Incognito was a play I really enjoyed, a stylised Alice in Wonderland, retaining Lewis Carroll's original characters but setting them in a modern context, it was a tragedy involving a drugs accompanied by lively club music.

Marie Galloway played a sweet Alice, trying to find her way though this surreal maze but tempted by characters around her. I loved writing the play and I have to say the kids were brilliant. Joining Marie on stage was Kerry Jackson Meek -who played her alter ego Syla. Mark Tunstall, the rap singing rabbit,was hilarious, Nick Saich, the gang boss in conflict with the Red Queen played by Eva Ferguson, a very formidable foe. In addition we also had Donna Kerr and Francesca Owen, Katie Grimwade, Simon Radford and Sam Dixon with Alice Bligh and quite a few supporting dancers. I would say it was ground breaking at the time. I was very pleased to be interviewed with Marie on BBC Radio Cambridgeshire Not only were this bunch great actors who never failed to deliver, but lovely people and a joy to work with. We had a very special relationship and I still keep in contact with some of them today But all good things come to an end and eventually this group moved on in the early nineties. There were new kids on the block, and they didn't disappoint either.

MARIE AND KERRY IN ALYS INCOGNIO

I wrote a play about animals performing in a circus, called *Performing Rights*. A group of protesters storm the ring with explosives and the animals escape. Derek actually directed this one and also designed the set with lions in a cage, and a circus ring. We also used jugglers from Eddie Konig's circus skills group who entered through the audience to bring alive the feeling of a real circus. Derek did a fabulous job as Director, we won the Adjudicator's prize at the Sawston drama festival. And by this time I was linking up with an English and drama teacher, Adrian Lockwood. And in 2002 we wrote and performed a play called *You Made Me*, about the effects of divorce and separation on children. Playing the lead was Helena Johnson, sister of Anna. Her younger sister in the performance was played by a newcomer in the group, eleven year old Frances Bowen Day. Choreography was by Stacey Dixon, who also played a social worker, and Faye Ferguson, sister of Eva . By this time I had a Literary agent, Rosemary Bromley, and Adrian and I were very pleased when it was published by HarperCollins Education. We performed the play at drama festivals but we were also honoured to be asked to perform it at Heydon Grange in front of thirty circuit court judges, to increase their understanding of issues affecting children going through legal conflicts and the heartbreak of families breaking up.

Channel 5 television also came down to film a segment with Sally Ann Kaiser for a teenage programme called T*he MAG.*

The play was also given splendid reviews by freelance writer Sue Elkin both in the Stage and the Times Literary supplement. What a result!

I also wrote a comedy for a change called *Goodbye Blackberry Way* about a boy Jack Ranner, growing up in the sixties, with reference to the Beatles, Coronation Street and Christine Keeler.

We won the prize for best junior group at the Cambridge Drama Festival.

In 2004 Adrian and I wrote our last play together, *Face Value,* published by Letts education, for schools and youth groups. This was about the effects of image on young people. We performed this during a PSHE day at Sawston and it was featured in the Daily Mail. It was great fun to perform. During our time of festivals we were often up against the wonderful work of local drama teacher and presenter Frances Brownlie, many of her talented young people came from the college and occasionally we had people in my group who were also competing in Frances' group, including my son Chris. Adrian, as Head of English, was finding it difficult to fit in play rehearsals and writing, same with me as Head of Year. Although we often talked about it, we have never written anything since.

But if I had to choose one piece of work above all else it would be an eco musical called *The Last Flower on Earth,* commissioned by Music Sales of Frith street,

London and published in 1995. I wrote the libretto and the music was composed by Cyril Ornadel, former BBC orchestra leader and Musical director at the London Palladium, working with many stars including Bruce Forsyth. Cyril also wrote the song *If I Ruled the World*. It was a shock for me though when I found out that in addition to the storyline and script I also had to write lyrics for the show, something I had never done before. It was a real challenge but I did it. Cyril was fantastic to work with. As he lived in Brighton, he only came up very occasionally but the musical was directed by Val Ford. I helped out with direction as did Cyril but this was Val's production and she did a fantastic job, not only with the cast but also persuading others from inside and outside the college, to give up their time, including Dorothy Abercrombie and David Leslie.

In the photo Cyril Ornadel composer with some of the cast

The musical was performed by several schools and it was great honour to watch the production of the South Lee school, Bury St Edmunds which took place at the wonderful Theatre Royal in Bury St Edmunds. Sue and I got to sit in the Royal box and I was introduced to the audience afterwards.Lady Mary Archer invited us as part of the National Garden scheme to perform the musical live in the gardens of her beautiful Old Rectory home in Grantchester. It was bit nerve wracking and not always easy for the cast to project their voices outside with no microphones. We were a main dancer down but Ceri Govan stepped in at the last moment and added to the scene by wearing red ribbons. But Lucy Barlow did a great job as musical director, helped as always by David Adams. Lord Archer came up to me after the performance and said 'That was a triumph old boy, a triumph.'

The main singing part went to Tory Harper, she had a beautiful voice, Kate Chesworth played Mother Earth, along with Mark Tunstall and Nick Saich who worked so well together, leading a chorus of about twenty pupils.

After the event the cast was invited to a strawberry and cream tea in the house, such a kind gesture, and I was very proud of our lovely students. An amazing time.

The Talent show 1984

This fabulous idea came from Janet Tomlin after I had moved to the Middle school. Janet was the deputy head. I hit it off instantly with Janet. We produced the show together, and I was very grateful to the choreographers and support of my friend and fellow tutor Graham Chivers. A lot of the organisation was done by the students themselves,. We had a fantastic number of pupils involved. Dancers, street dancers, break dancers, jazz ballet group, and four fantastic talented gymnasts performing their routine in a confined space on stage

Our neighbour, Hayley Bridges and Melanie Woods sang as Caged Birds, there were comedy sketches, including Roland Rat and a martial arts karate expert smashing blocks of wood bravely held by Graham! And even before Britain's Got Talent we got a performing dog on stage, a lovely German shepherd called Sheba,who jumped through hoops, plus an hilarious moment when Lindsay Brunnock and Jackie Green left the stage and came into the audience. (See later section on TV and Film)

I was enormously proud of them all. Only problem was the show took place in the middle of a teachers' industrial action, this wasn't happening when we first started rehearsing. Teachers in one union were 'working to rule' withdrawing from lunch time duties and not doing anything outside basic lessons. I did have some sympathy but I've only ever took action on one occasion, withdrawing lunchtime supervision. However, during this course of action some teachers refused to support any out of school activities or carry out any tasks beyond teaching lessons. That's their right, but I was disappointed when some teachers refused to hand out tickets for the show, even to children in their own form, during registration, tickets which had been processed in the office. That's all they had to do, hand out envelopes to the children. I thought this was petty and vindictive. But the Middle school office, led by secretary Jean Walker, did a fabulous job in collecting the money and issuing the tickets to support not just Janet and myself, but all the wonderful performers who gave up their time, some of whom had never been on stage before. It was a great show and the parents too were so supportive. And to be fair, quite a few staff did come along to support us. If there's a show or school play coming up the first thing students say to their teachers is 'Are you coming to watch?' It means so much to each and every individual who participates I have kept a special VHS tape recorded on the night which is very precious.

I was so proud of all them all.

Two of the gymnasts, Juliet and Kate

SHEBA ON STAGE
She was the perfect act, stepping through hoops and really enjoying herself, She was so friendly, a lovable member of cast!

The Teen Commandments was the title of my first published play by Oxford University Press in 1992, it was performed in several schools in the UK and also in the Australian outback on the radio Very proud of that!

Katie Dermendjieva (Grimwade) and Nick Saich

The photos in the book were of my group posing in

dramatic situations around Sawston VC photographed by Paul Morris.

Eva Ferguson, Kerry Meek Jackson, Nick Saich and Mark Tunstall
A scene from the Teen Commandments

The best drama always invoves conflict!

We sometimes used drama in PSHE lessons, drawings and photos used as teaching aids. Here is one example. This is **Katie Crawford** playing a victim of bullying in Year Nine, this was played out on a storyboard. They really were her best friends! With Lucy Kerr and Eleanor and I think Anna.
Copies would be made for all classes in that year group

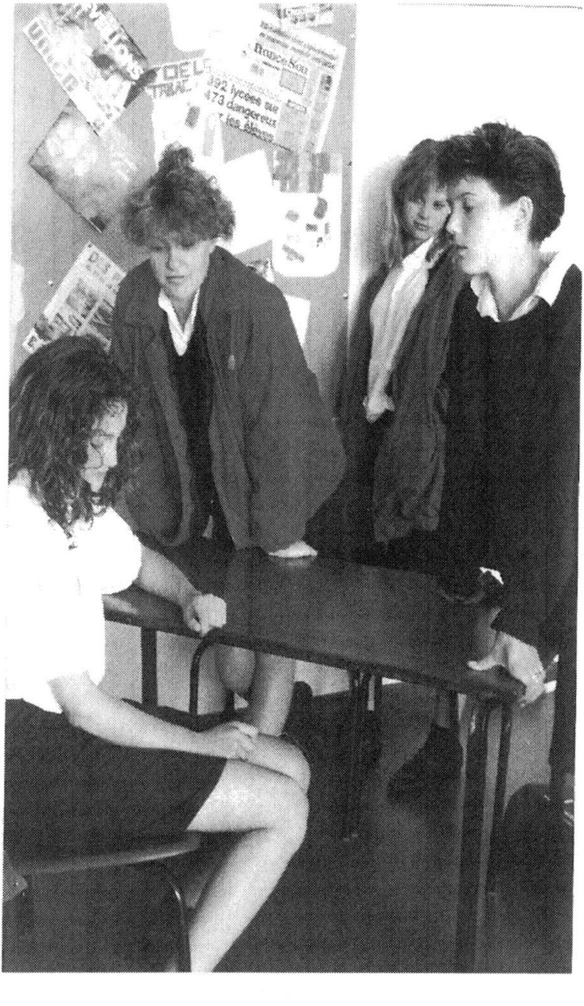
392 lycées sur
473 dangereux

Chapter Twenty One

Being Charlie Waite

In 2012 although retired, I returned as a supply teacher and took over a Year 11 form in the Spicer wing. Most mornings when I arrived early to set up my lessons for the day, Phoebe Waite would be there already having been dropped off earlier. It was always good to chat with Phoebe, we often talked books we were reading and occasionally she helped to put together the weekly form quiz. Phoebe said there were too many questions on football! When I left that group at Christmas, Phoebe gave me a lovely tin of biscuits and a card thanking me for being her form teacher. We became friends on facebook when she went to University but then I lost contact with her and assumed she wasn't on facebook any more, until a few months ago. The mystery was explained.

'I met Mr Reynolds when I was in year 7 and he was teaching us about the Black Death in history, it became one of my favourite topics after that. Throughout my time at SVC, I had the pleasure of being taught by him many more times, including when he was our cover form tutor in year 11. Form time was great, Mr Reynolds was always so kind and really interested in what we had to say, we'd have great class discussions about anything and everything, including the peacock that used to roam around the school and our favourite books.

During SVC, I was female-presenting and I had no idea what a trans person was (I wouldn't until I went to university) but I did know that I was different. Had I been able to explore my gender identity earlier, my mental health issues may have manifested differently as I journeyed through puberty and education settings. I came out as bisexual around age 13 and this didn't seem to be a problem at the time but I now remember a lot of bi phobic comments from other students (including friends) as well as a lot of sexist jokes from male peers. All of this was very usual for the time and I didn't consider it bullying at all, however, I can now see how my view of myself as a teenager was impacted by this environment.

I came out as non binary in 2020 and was referred under the NHS for gender affirming care, I am still on a waiting list for an initial appointment 3 years later. The following year, I came out as a transgender man, changed my name and pronouns socially and sought hormone treatment privately. After coming out as man, societally ingrained gender norms made me feel like I couldn't engage with anything 'feminine' any more (like painting my nails or wearing eyeliner), so I spent a long time in baggy t-shirts and cargo trousers. Now, however, I live as a non-binary transmasculine person and I try not to worry about what is considered masculine or feminine and just express myself in whatever feels comfortable.

This year, after a lot of saving and fundraising, I hope to have top surgery privately which will greatly help with my dysphoria. I recognise that I am very privileged to be able to access any gender affirming treatment at all and this is not the case for so many transgender people.'

I would like to thank Charlie for sharing his journey with us and wish him all the very best for the future.

CHARLIE WAITE

Chapter Twenty Two

My Kind of People (1)

Please understand I cannot remember every single event or include every person, from 1975 to 2017, this is just a random selection from some of the people who have been in my year groups, my classes, and who worked in my productions or sent me messages on Facebook.

The Tomlinsons namely.....Samantha, Michelle, Emma, Danielle, Samantha, Rebecca. Ashleigh, and Rachel who was in my year group and one boy, Josh.

Rachel, recorded a song in a video workshop playing Marianne Faithful and sang *As Tears Go By,* A superb cover!

Rachel went to work in a school, in fact all the family have done well. Samantha is now manager of a hostel in Cambridge for young homeless girls. What a brilliant thing to do. Recently young Jade achieved the first part of a degree. They are a great family, kind and loving, who stick together and support each other, this shines through in their posts on social media which shows how much family means to each and everyone of them. And you know, they never forget my birthday on Facebook. Fantastic family. Here's two of them...Sam and Rachel!

Issy Baker, our production assistant on a school video, went on to to work as a riding instructor and now runs her own veterinary physiotherapy practice in Colchester.

IZZY BAKER

Amanda. I don't recall her other name but she kept ferrets at home and on one of our show and tell history lessons, she brought them in for us all to see. (Not quite sure where the history came into it but every now again, like Charlotte and her sheep, it was good to hear about pupils' interests outside the classroom. We had so much fun with those ferrets, they were very friendly and easy to handle. We pushed the desks together and constructed a little race track with pencil cases as fences and the ferrets raced each other. Of course none of this would be allowed today in school!

Lauren Hills When she was at school Lauren took a liking to my MX5, and always asked to buy it. I don't think she ever got an MX5 but I did see a picture of her sitting astride a very powerful motor cycle. Lauren was popular girl, I believe she now works in farming.

Freya Walkley. (Vaughan)

I first came across Freya at Duxford school, visiting as Head of Year to talk to the Year 6 class coming to the college. Actually it was my birthday and as I entered the classroom Freya stood up, wished me a happy birthday and led the whole class singing it. That was a first meeting with a difference, still don't know how she found out. Freya was a great girl at SVC, she and her best friend, Lucy Argent. were in Terry Saunders' form close to my office, not a day went past when they didn't come and say good morning. Freya and Lucy were also good at organising events, Lucy's dad was an agent I believe, they put on a couple of shows to raise money for charity and the Year 11 prom. Freya and her friends also organised a fabulous dance and fashion show for charity to support our student Laurinda Jaffrey, who contacted meningitis and was absent from school for many weeks. It was wonderful that Laurinda was able to take part in that show. Plus Freya did a lot of work for the trip to Disneyland. We went on the saucers together which was my limit after experiencing the runaway train. When she left Freya gave me a beautifully designed cup engraved with my name, and underneath it says 'Thanks. Freya.' Indeed, thanks Freya for all you did. I chose Freya for the student of the year award in 2001. Freya went to work in hospitality and as an events manager. One day I met her in town near King's College when she was on lunch break. Unfortunately a group of students were protesting, can't remember what exactly it was about but there was a heavy police presence and all the protesters were ushered into an area near the Senate house. Unfortunately, Freya and I got caught up in this as we were chatting. I thought we were going to be arrested but fortunately after a few minutes we managed to get away. Another Freya moment to cherish. We still keep in contact on Facebook and I still refer to her as my Head girl!

Those who helped with the year book included Kayleigh Paske, Nicola Simpson, who also presented me with a signed photo alongside Anneka Daley and Jenny Cameron, Naomi Bryant, Anna Brown, Line dancer Lizzie Shiels and Sam Leonard. Not forgetting Kirk Northrop, what a character. Guy Chisholm, Ed Knowles, Adam Sistig. Kelly Gouldthorp, Phil Doggett commended in maths, Sam Tanner, Suzie Bullivant, Sarah Bellis who did go on to follow her dream and work in the aircraft industry Kim who didn't go on to follow her dream to become a WWE wrestler but did very well in other ways.

John Hutchison, always smiling, never gave up. Sue gave him a lot of support as his TA at school.

Hana Moezzeni who wanted to become a writer but later became a very talented artist. She once gave me tea in her garden in Duxford.

Natalie Tendai, when we first met I recall her reading a magazine about fashion and music. She loved fashion and music, still does, what a livewire. Now lives near Warrington, I think. Her morning posts on facebook always brighten my day. Hilarious! Told her she should be a comedian and I am pleased that we are still in contact. Only found out recently that Natalie Is still good friends with Lauranda who I mentioned in the paragraph above. I imagine they have some fun together!

Natalie Tendai

Sam Foakes, a trick cyclist. he was very good and he performed on the very last day of the year group in 2001 in our farewell assembly.

Tom Kelk and Sophie Wiesner. 2001-2006. I used to teach Tom's mum, Sarah. Tom will always be remembered for his 'Sex Bomb' Tom Jones impersonation in Pop idol, fantastic. He also did a very funny boy band sketch with Jack Bradley and Matthew Drury, this lot were always willing to help out with shows and assemblies. Sophie and Tom got together in year 10, and remained that way through University before getting married a few years ago. Sophie was a splendid support to the year group and I chose her as 2006 Girl of the Year, and saying 'Sophie is always smiling, the happiest girl I know.'

I was torn originally between Sophie and Freya Chaplin, because she too did a huge amount to help and inspire this year group. In the end, judgement of Solomon, I gave her the award as well. Not forgetting *Mark Baslington* who won the male award. Mark was always there to advise on technology and in charge of lighting and sound for our shows. A splendid young man, always calm and friendly.

Also that year we had the wonderful 'Hot For Jack' an all girl group, Clare Lampon, Maryam Oghanna and Jessica Lilley. who played in many concerts to support our year group and revues. I played and sang with them on stage a couple of times which was good fun and I put the group in my first fiction kindle book.

Two I could always rely on were the twins Emily and Francesca White, both brilliant dancers but always there to speak up for others. Their mum a lovely, humorous person.

Jenny Collier was head of St Albans school and her daughter Charlie, herself now a teacher, was in my year. When Jenny had her 60th we were invited to her party with Charlie and her friends from my year group.

Dawn Newman. For a short time I taught her older sister Catherine, a quiet, lovely girl then Dawn arrived! Dawn is a real character and she was fun to teach. She was quite friendly with my eldest Shane and his mates in Sawston for a time when they were teenagers. I recall one evening, it might have been Halloween , when flour bombs burst around the street and hit our wall. Never did find out who it was! Later Dawn returned to the college in the canteen so it was lovely to see her when I was on supply. Since leaving the college for a second time Dawn went into the care section. I think this an ideal job for Dawn, I know she's brilliant at this as she recently won a very special award.

Anna Holt Tenberg a remarkable young lady at the college and a fabulous dancer. She asked me to help her once to produce a show to raise money for her year group. I was a mere spectator, Anna was the producer and did a great job. She then choreographed the *Mama*

Mia routine with the staff for one Christmas show, that was fabulous. Loved that. A kind, thoughtful, caring girl and a joy to work with at the college. Anna takes up the story

'I also remember choreographing a Jive for the PE department,
they did lifts and everything to Alesha Dixon, the Boy Does Nothing! We put on lots of performances and fundraising. In the early days after leaving college I danced in competitions such as the British National Championships, European Championships and World Championships in Latin American Formation Dancing. I have performed at The Blackpool Opera House and Cambridge University, as well as performing for both the British and Russian Royal families.
I now have my own Performing Arts Academy, teaching dance, Acrobatics, Musical Theatre as well as Adult Salsa, Ballroom and Latin and Fitness Classes I absolutely adore teaching and sharing my passion for dance, fitness and performing arts.'

I recall throughout the pandemic Anna kept dancing and every morning went through routines, on facebook always positive and smiling and encouraging everyone. Sometimes her little daughter Willow tried to join in, so funny to watch.

ANNA HOLT (TENBERG)

Maheen Sattar. A quiet and friendly girl in my year group of 2006 and one of the few Muslim girls in the school at that time. Maheen was always tolerant of others but equally always true to her faith. For example she came on the trip to Spain and joined in all activities and visits except one. We had a little disco party on the last night. Although she enjoyed herself she wouldn't go onto the floor even though her friends were all encouraging her. She smiled and stayed seated. I admired her for that. During festivals, she would bring sweets and share with other children in her form. And one occasions if she needed a quiet and private place for lunchtime prayers, I let her use my office. Maheen is now working and we keep in contact on Facebook.

Jamie Peck, unforgettable rendition of an England football song in our pop idol competition! Jamie also helped members of year 8 plant the first daffodils along Hillside, around 2002, with help and support of others, including Margaret Badcock. They are still in bloom today.

Others who stand out who were not in my year group. Two of my history students who both told me in Year 8 that they wanted to be history teachers!

Cassie Cope I knew I was getting close to retirement when Cassie asked if she could use Movie maker to do a presentation to the rest of the class on 19th century medicine. I had never used it, and didn't know how to. It was brilliant. Cassie also acted and helped in drama productions, along with her friend Fiona Jackson. Cassie went on to gain a place at Jesus College, Cambridge before starting her career as a history teacher at Chesterton Community College.

Fiona Case told me at parents evening in year 8 that she wanted to be a history teacher Her work was always immaculate, detailed and showed great understanding of the subject. she succeeded in her ambition both at Saffron Walden County High and Linton VC.

Karen Salter Poole and Christine Poole. Sadly they lost their dad when they were very young, but both girls went on to achieve great things. Karen was a regular member of the youth centre group, a talented singer and actress. She also helped on the production of Last Flower. Later Karen worked in childcare and became the manager of a Nursery in Tannery Road Sawston, rated outstanding by Ofsted. Recently she became a radio presenter on Burwell radio.

Christine really did follow the dream. She worked with Adrian and I in the You Made Me stage production at SVC where she played the silent One. Later she studied at Mountview Academy of arts, and went on to work in many professional productions, music and drama projects, cruise ships, and other venues abroad. Both wonderful girls who have achieved so much, always encouraged by their lovely mum, Carol. Their dad would have been so proud of them.

Alan Gleaves seems to be doing a lot of touring recently overseas which is great and puts up pictures of himself playing the guitar, I don't remember him in a band at school but he is obviously enjoying himself now!

David Todd one of the earlier seventies students. David made friends with me on facebook, he was always a very good student, with a good sense of humour. Loves football, I believe his son is now a referee. Things have been very tough for David over recent months but he always finds something amusing and positive to say,

Ruth, Johnny and Lucy Munden

Ruth was in my class in the seventies when she was in year 8, she had a road accident and broke her leg and spent some time in Addenbrooke's Hospital. The rest of the class got a card and signed it and I visited Ruth in hospital and took her some sweets, Some years later Ruth returned to the college as a Science teacher and I didn't recognise her until she reminded me of the accident and my hospital visit. Ruth's children came to the college and Jonny was in my year group. Jonny married Lucy Warner. Lucy, after an apprenticeship, now runs her own business Lucy Warner Hair in Stapleford. I interviewed her on my Radio show and we did an Elton John duet as he is one of Lucy's favourite artists.

Ruth, like me,has retired now but we met her and her husband at Wandlebury taking their dog for a walk on two occasions. It's a small world isn't it?

Tina Beards. And still on the subject of hairdressers Tina has been running her own business for 29 years now in Sawston, starting when she was fourteen and still seeing some of her original clients she started with. Tina was a delightful pupil and I caught up with her at John Marven's funeral. It's really good to see people like Tina using their skills and determination to start and maintain their own business in the locality.

Clare Driver. A farmer's daughter who has maintained her love for nature and the environment. A campaigner for all animals and insects, she is also active in her community of Ickleton. But I remember her most as a student who loved history and I am thrilled that she still loves the subject, I am so pleased that I could inspire Clare when she was at the college. Clare, on more than one occasion, has sent me messages of support saying I helped her during a difficult time when she was at school. This means a lot to me. I have included one of Clare's messages at the end.

Catriona Love (Davidson) Catriona was in my history class from a young age but I really got to know her when she studied medicine as part of the Schools History project for GCSE. Catriona said she wanted to be a doctor, key reason being that she had suffered from quite severe asthma attacks since she was little. Her work was exceptional and it was a joy having Catriona in my class, but all her teachers had to be aware that asthma attacks can happen very quickly. One morning Catriona didn't look very well, I asked if she wanted to go outside but she said she was OK, but having witnessed my own son having a bad asthma attack, I knew the signs and potential consequences. When I could see Catriona's condition was worsening, I ran to the office next door and dialled 999. Medical help arrived from the main office immediately. Her Dad was also notified. Fortunately, the medics were able to stabilise her condition and she returned to school, I believe, the next day.

And I was thrilled when Catriona gained an A* in history and went on to achieve her ambition and studied medicine at Newcastle, before becoming a doctor at Addenbrooke's Hospital. I am very proud of Catriona, now married with children. Her husband is former student Sam Love. And the last time we spoke online the asthma attacks had declined in their severity.

The day she left Catriona gave me a card which I have treasured, I read it there and then, it was so beautiful thanking me for looking after her and inspiring her to achieve her goal. The only time that a card from a pupil has left me with tears in my eyes. Catriona featured in my first kindle book You Made Me, where she played a fictional part as herself, known as Dr Cat, and also advised on medical examinations in hospital. An amazing girl.

George Baglin. George was a real character at school, popular and engaging. He supported some of our shows and on one occasion compared Pop Idol. He wrote his own script and Gerry Holloway wasn't keen on him doing that and asked me to keep an eye on what he was intending to say. He was fine, usual introductions to competitors done with humour and clarity. And then came Grace Mooney, already a regular performer in our shows. George asked Grace what number she was about to sing and when she told him he said 'Ah, yes I heard you were singing that song in the shower this morning,' to which Grace replied

'Well, you should know George, you were there.' I tried to avoid looking at Gerry on the other side of the stage! I have to say it went down very well and showed a great sense of humour on Grace and George's part. Oh and as far as I'm aware it wasn't true!

George had an older brother, Tom, who I think played football in Dave's team. He also had three sisters, two of which came to the college. Lucy was the eldest, she acted in drama productions when she was in year 7 and 8 then went to work as cabin crew with Virgin Airways, travelling all over the world.

Clare Baglin was in my history group for three years. She wrote one of the best slave diaries in Yr 9 I've ever seen. She did beautiful work but could be a bit chatty at times, and I told some of her friends at lunchtime there was to be a new seating plan in history that afternoon and I would be moving some people around. The plan was on my desk and somehow during lunch break it disappeared. I never saw it again. I was convinced Clare had found it or one or her friends, but of course, they all denied it! Clare did exceptionally well in her studies and I last saw her at Steve Mastin's 40th birthday dinner at a restaurant in Cambridge. Clare came up and spoke to me. I didn't recognise her at first, such an elegant and articulate young lady. She was with her parents and I went over and had a brief chat with them. I think they are both doctors. They were full of praise for the staff and the college and it's lovely to see how much the Baglins have achieved in their lives since leaving school.

Teresa and Elisa Turner Mother and daughter, lively and friendly students, friends on facebook and I thank them for their kind messages of support over the years and the faith they had in my teaching This means a lot to me. Likewise Teresa's friend Sonia Ellis, another very pleasant pupil, always smiling.

Hayley Galvin such a lovely student to work with. She always had ambitions to form a church on the border between Northern and Southern Ireland, not sure she managed to do that but she did go on to become an RE teacher. Hayley was always a good friend of Fran Bowen Day. She was and is a great singer, a regular member of Youth Centre productions. Hayley took part in the Talent 2000 contest as well as singing *My Heart Will Go On* as a surprise for Sue at her fiftieth birthday party at the Red Lion, Whittlesford. She could play any role with talent and enthusiasm and it's great that she is still performing with her own jazz group I believe, down in Hampshire. Sue and I took her and Fran to see Britney Spears in London.

Cheryl Rush danced in our first college video *Chain Reaction* and what a superb dancer! Cheryl went on to compete in lots of national competitions and shows. Sadly, her dancing career came to an abrupt end owing to a debilitating illness that affected her life and still does. But I have to say that Cheryl always tries to remain positive, even though she's endured so many operations and visits to A and E at Addenbrooke's. Cheryl always comes back smiling, she values so much family life and adores her two lovely children. Cheryl, you truly are an inspiration.

Cheryl's best friend at SVC was Emma Ward who was our babysitter for a time as well as working on productions. Together they were both very trendy, like designer year sevens! Emma went on to become a professional photographer.

Paul Cage I only caught up with him in recent times when he sent me a friend request on facebook. Paul's postings usually involve what he is cooking, his love of football and the next adventure he is planning with Freya. Its lovely to see them sharing so many good times together, Paul is another example of someone with a purpose and positive attitude to life.

Hayley Bridges my next door neighbour. I guess it can be quite awkward if you live next door to your teacher which happened when we moved to Princess Drive in 1978. Dick and Julie were excellent neighbours, we became good friends and would meet from time to time for drinks and a BBQ. And the kids were fine, calling me Kelvin but once they stepped through the college gates it was always Mr Reynolds. Daryl was an excellent footballer and Hayley was a singer and dancer who took part in our Talent show. I recall on one occasion we took her on a day out with our kids to Colchester Zoo and the car overheated so Hayley and I scrambled down a bank to find a stream and fill up a plastic bottle of water. Another time I'd got one of those helium balloons and wanted to see how high it would fly, so Hayley got a cotton reel and we tied it around the balloon. It went up really high but then when we tried to reel it in the cotton cable snared on an aerial across the road and got stuck. I never did tell the them! Also in Princess Dive we once had a torrential downpour and the drains overflowed and the kids came into the street to paddle. The water was knee high. Hayley, following in her mum's footsteps, works as a hairdresser in the village. When I returned to SVC as a supply teacher I taught one of Daryl's boys and and Hayley's daughter Deanna, was in my Year 11 form.

Babysitters. I always had a good choice of pupils available who I trusted and I have to say they all did a fantastic job for all three of my children. Usually it was just a couple of hours for a meal out for Sue and I, but so much appreciated. Apart from Hayley, Kerry Smith, Emma Ward, Stephanie Osborne, Justine Reeve, Kathryn Badcock. And I think our last one was **Antoinette Blundell Bonelli,** who I taught in Year 11. Once Chris was poorly and Sue wasn't keen to go out but Antoinette insisted we went and said it would be fine. And it was. Thank you to all of you for allowing us a little bit of peace and an occasional night out!

In Teversham Way we lived for a time next to the Diplock family who had two children at the college. One day when dad was away, a mouse appeared in their living room and went down the back of the sofa. Mum was petrified and asked if I could come round to find the mouse, I was reminded of this recently when I met Laura in Tesco, she's now a teacher with children of her own. I don't think we ever did find the mouse but the sofa was pretty much ruined!

Anastasia Harebloom? Something, quite a title but I know who she is, she read my book *She's Not There* and was petrified by the falling lift scene! Always interested in history, now runs a BB in Norfolk and member of the local community.

Andy Ahmad- Cooke has his own music show on Music Galaxy Radio a writer and producer at several companies.

Jessica Ruth appeared in our school video Blue Twilight, sitting on a picnic bench with Poppy Gaye and Helena Johnson. Now a zoo keeper in the Midlands with children of her own.

Kirsty Anne Fell studied animal care at the college of

west Anglia works in healthcare, her sister Collette, lives in the USA and helped with our play *Face Value.*

Adam Murray, a very good footballer who once reminded me that my tax disc on my car was a week out of date! I kept checking regularly after that! A lovely lad, Adam's dad is TV presenter and former Cambridge United and Manchester United footballer, Dion Dublin.

Georgia Taylor was in my Year 8 class on March 14th celebrating her thirteenth birthday, when I got a call to say that my second grandson Joel had been born couple of hours earlier. Now she's grown up Georgia always sends a birthday greeting to Joel on their birthdays. Great girl!

Amber Lenaghan, we are related through the Reynolds rock family and I didn't know for some time but I still see her working in Ely on occasions and we always have a joke about school, she's done very well and I'm proud of my second cousin, now she has a little girl of her own.

Lucy French did a fantastic job one day in RE when Ofsted came in, helping distribute books and worksheets. so pleased they looked at her exercise book and she answered all the questions! Top girl.

Christine Wilcox part of the 1978 community, often seems to be at music concerts, always positive.

Lauren Dunk, only recently made friends with me, her dad Lol worked as a caretaker for many years at SVC.

Tracy Fabb, a kind girl at school and I'm sure she's still the same, her posts are always positive and helpful and funny at times.

Glenn Wright, seems to enjoy travelling, interesting guy and he invited me to join the Sawston Community group on Facebook which has been useful

Marnie Robins, after one very rainy day Marnie let me share her umbrella, I think I got the lion's share haha, recall singing that song 'Umbrella Ella' and I never let her forget that. I'm sure she got fed up with that joke but she was always smiling.

Kerri Lightning regular and interesting poster on Facebook, comes from one of the traditional Sawston families/

Amy Duthie- Smith went from my room H3 to Queensland, back to her home country. Byron Bay where I know she is having a pretty cool life.

Graham Andrade very fit and active man according to his FB posts, park runs and cycling. Puts me to shame!

Juliet Cooper- Chinnick now Jules, small girl but very athletic, an award winning gymnast will feature in the sporting section of the next book, part of a group including Susie Nichols and Kate Latham Lawson.

Sabrina Young, hilarious posts about her children. Always amusing and sensitive young lady.

Kerry Daly recently paid me a compliment when she was on holiday visiting the ancient sites in Greece recently, saying how much she enjoyed the ancient history course.

Anna Mortlock has I believed moved into Burwell although I haven't met her in the street

Lewis Mitcham, always popular lad with a lot of talent and interest in the Youth centre productions,

Steve Williams, does so much to help with production on Marven centre musicals, great that someone is willing to give up so much of he time to help the kids' productions,

Gabi Collins, mad on Argentina and especially Lionel Messi, something we shared in common, as you will see from a previous chapter.

Jackie Garrick, kind and thoughtful girl, always smiling left to return to Hong Kong I think, we're stil friends on fbook.

Sanjay Mistry, think he was friends with Chris back in the day, always seems to be out with his family for meals, he's probably a trip advisor!

Sam Tanner, excellent student in my year and his mum worked at the college,

*Chris Bake*r, also had an interest in drama and the arts, returned as a member of staff for a time

Beth Hicks, show jumper and photographer and her sister Jess who studied drama and music, now performs her own one woman shows, Brilliant combination.

Lydia Chantler-Hicks, very funny girl once during a sponsored mile walk round the field for charity, with her friend Sarah, Lydia insisted on wearing my brown anorak with a fur collar, don't ask me why, here's the proof

Twins *Chloe and Lydia Hamilton,* Lydia went on to study at Goldsmith's London where I once had a place and Chloe who told me she wanted to be a writer, achieved that dream, writing for the I national newspaper and interviewing many interesting and famous pople before leaving journalism behind and turning instead to teaching English at Impington VC.

Tasha Cole, poster girl for my first kindle book and then went on to model for a time, before graduating in science

Helen Brinkworth, lived just around the corner from us in Princess Drive, she was a very good pupil and when we moved in Helen came round to help unpack with her friend Angela, and to look after Shane who was only eight months old. Some years later when Becca Baker started working at Cambridge University Press Helen was her line manager.

Sarah Myers. Became Manager of a playgroup in Suffolk, now has a child of her own. Here's was One classic history trip to Berlin, Sarah was so tired she fell asleep against the Berlin Wall holding her teddy bear!

Flossie Mills(Maltby) a real character, pictured earlier with the group, worked as a paramedic.

Anthony Osborne has kept in contact on facebook with me and also many others from his year group.

Emma Saunders, occasionally exchange reading ideas, taught Emma's daughter at Linton.

Rachel Whittle, I think she knew more about RE than I did,! Fabulous work, dad was a minister in the free Church I think.

Fay Ferguson part of my drama group, excellent dancer, sister of Eva.

Sebastian Murray studied medicine and is now a senior anaesthetist at a London hospital, I know this because my nephew Jonny, who didn't come to the college, is also an anaesthetist and by coincidence worked with Sebastian.

Vicky Reynolds-Cocroft, no relation , went to work for the NHS and is also a great campaigner. *Lauren Blencowe*, Vicky's friend, used to joke that she would work in a firework factory, I don't think she did but I know that Lauren wrote a book that was published about a gluten free diet.

Laura Walker, very active from her posts in local community in *Saffron Walden,* always positive and smiling.

Sophie Day in my last form, never did make those chocolate cakes!

Alex Cracknell Really supportive member of my year group

Hannah Prowse, when I asked the class if they had ever met any one famous, Hannah said her granddad was in Star Wars, he played the original Darth Vader! That was true, the legendary David Prowse

Suzie Bullivant. Fair to say we didn't always see eye to eye in Year 9 and I didn't always think I handled situations well, but we worked out an agreement and built a relationship, and the last two years were brilliant. Suzie started her own business after leaving school and we have met a couple of times over the years, she now has a little girl of her own, and we stilll keep in contact on facebook.

The Nichols girls Sarah, Suzie, Amelia and Gemma, all excellent members of the school community. Their lovely mum Elaine looked after my David in the premature unit at the Rosie hospital when he was born in 1987. She even wrote him a funny report on his progress when he was discharged, which we still have. Very sad for the family when Elaine passed away a few years later.

And not forgetting Clare Bear, Clare Louise, Sarah Noble, Steph Coulson,Adam Grange, Penny Grange, Gemma Bastick, Gemma Groves, Charlene Gillet, Becky Dunn. Becky Barton, Gavin Murray, new boy on the block Steven Satchell, Amy Jarvis, Sarah Baker, Laura West, Mary Silley, Olwyn Jones, Mark Ellis, Amie Govan,Laura Murray, Emily Upton, Emily Greenwood,Molly Clark, Michele King,.Alison Start, I think she's now at the King Bill out at Heydon way, haven't been there for years. Naomi Arnold, Mark

Woodstock, Taylor Addison and Jessica. Michelle King, Anna Genevier, Yasmin Mackay, Emma Fearon, Tanya and Kerry Jones, Chloe Brand, Georgia Record. Laura Maling, Laura Dartnell, Laura West and all my Facebook friends from Sawston.

And a big shout out to those who acted brilliantly in Face Value and were featured in the Daily Mail.
Kehl Nugent, Tatyana Orrock, Sam Tilling and James Sharpe
Maya Bienz, fabulous member of my year group who gave great advice to my nephew Johnny when he was applying to study medicine at UCL, especially interview techniques. Thank you Maya,

And finally in memory of dear Charlie Poole who was so brave and positive to the end.

****

Impossible to remember and name everyone but there will be an opportunity for some former students to contribute to a memory board in the next book scheduled for next year. Apologies if I didn't get your name entirely correct,. There have been a few changes over the years!

Drama award winners Francesca Owen and Sally Whitaker presented by Lady Mary Archer

Chapter Twenty Three

Being Stacey Dixon

I last met Stacey in the Robin Hood Inn, Cambridge (not the picture above) taking her children for a meal. Lovely to see her again. On supply at SVC I taught her daughter, just as helpful and talented as her mum. Stacey had a speaking part in You Made Me, in addition to sharing the choreography and was also featured in Channel 5's The Mag.

But It was after she left school that Stacey became a model and then joined the wonderful and glamorous world of pageantry when her life took on a whole new meaning. Stacey tells her story:

'I was first introduced to pageantry through a contact from the modelling agency I was signed with back in 2006. I was told it was a great way to 'get your face out there'.

I blindly stepped out onto the stage, completely clueless to the true magnitude of pageantry, every outfit was wrong, my walk was wrong and oblivious to what my 'platform' should be - I thought it was a type of shoe!

But none the less I fell in love with the sisterhood amongst the girls, and very quickly realised these women were dedicated to raising awareness for causes close to their hearts, raising money for charities, and genuinely trying to implement a positive change in the world.

Does it sound corny? Yes it does, but they really did all want world peace, it felt like I'd found a missing piece to my puzzle and I was determined to learn more about this world and to fully embrace this new found hobby. Unsurprisingly I didn't place in this first pageant, I did however make lifelong friends, one of whom was actually my bridesmaid several years later.

I am often met with negativity when telling new people not only that I'm involved with the Pageant community but three of my children have also competed and held titles, they have images of the TV show 'Toddlers and Tiaras' or recall horror stories such as the one of Jon Benet Ramsey but I don't judge others for their opinions, it's simply a case of not knowing any different, and I'm always happy to educate and explain just what it is I do.

I have raised thousands of pounds for charities, Great Ormond street children's hospital, Brain Tumour research, The Christy, and Addenbrooke's charitable trust to name just a few, as well as organisations mass donations to support organisations such as Smalls for All, Soles for Soles, Trussel trust food banks and Blue Cross.

I have held regional, national and international titles throughout my pageant journey, and have travelled around the world representing the United Kingdom, the most memorable to date was being flown to Las Vegas to represent the UK in the Mrs Earth pageant, I earned the international title of Mrs Earth Eco that year, which was a huge honour.

The on stage performance is only a small snippet of the true journey involved with being a title holder, it's thrilling, nerve racking and sometimes scary, but in that moment everything you've worked for comes together.

From an outsider perspective it may appear we just stand on stage with glamorous gowns, big hair and bold makeup, but we also behind the scenes are interviewed, our knowledge of various world events, our platform (our chosen charities and awareness campaigns to support) as well as hobbies and hopes are discussed.

It is my belief that pageants have had a positive effect on mine and my familiy's lives. My youngest daughter, who now 13 has competed since she was four, is able to talk clearly and with confidence to a room full of others, through her interview training, she will engage with peers and wants to make a difference to this world as do all my children.'

What a wonderful experience, and as Stacey says it's helping her own children as well. A fantastic achievement and I am certain that Stacey still has lots more to offer.

Stacey winning Miss United Kingdom Earth and on the way to Las Vegas International Final

Stacey with daughter Amelia and Lily-May

Young competitors, helping build confidence, fund raising and having fun!

Chapter Twenty Four

My Kind of People (2)

Jo Nash Redfarn Was the reason for the introduction of Ancient History due to her love of the subject and her determination. Will feature in the next book including history, Jo was a successful manager of the Red House Nursery in Burwell for a number of years, her passsion for vintage aircraft and history continues.

Alison Spicer 'right back at yer' Riess.' What a character. I believe she played an Emperor in the first pantomime I worked on in 1975, Alison now lives in Canada. She does a lot of drama promoting her local groups, always busy, still keeps in contact with former students and staff, Allie. remembers my lovely platform shoes from 1975 (they were awful!)

Vanessa Cross. Danced in our Chain Reaction video. Such a talented background, not surprising that she soon established her own dance group expanding to many other locations in the county, not only on a weekly basis but also special workshops during holiday times. Vanessa returned to the college to teach GCSE dance, and we worked together on a special charity show a few years back with her dance group and a Britney Spears tribute act, played by Sarah, one of Vanessa's dance teachers at the time. Vanessa's love of dance is such an inspiration to her students and she never fails to promote their achievements. She is a fantastic teacher and motivator. The last few months have been a very sad time for Vanessa losing her husband Nick,who passed away last year. Vanessa has shown tremendous strength and even in the darkest days will always find something positive to say on social media. An amazing lady.

Emma Cracknell was in my 2001-2006 year group, so it was very surprising when she returned to the college as a Learning support teacher, before becoming a drama teacher. Emma is a lovely person to work with, and we still keep in contact.

Tracy Fitzpatrick was the star of my history group a few years back, but returned as as science technician during which she also found time to help with production on a couple of plays. Sunday mornings Tracy would be on the football pitch supporting her son who played in the same team as David. Tracy now works in the national health section. But I can guarantee she will always have a smile on her face.

Jazz Greenwood has just retired from the NHS and received a long service award after spending over 20 years working as a nurse at the Royal Papworth hospital. What an achievement!

Kelly Robertson and Jo Bishop from 1996, friends and excellent students never gave me any bother, always tried hard always pleasant. Kelly too suffered a loss when her mum Sally, who I remember when she was at school, passed away suddenly far too early.

Sarah Driscoll from the same year group was always willing to help tidy up Miss Boaz' form room, so reliable. Delighted that she became a Chelsea supporter, although our team's fortunes have changed over the last two seasons we hope for better things and still exchange views on facebook about Chelsea's latest results. Bring back Jose Mourinho, eh Sarah?

Mary Handley really liked history but she wasn't in my year group. But I think she also supports Cambridge United. During the pandemic she walked every single day whatever the weather through the villages of West Suffolk, between 2020 and 2022, She even made time to visit the graves of my ancestors and a war memorial for my great uncle in Hundon Church, where my grandmother came from.

Nicola Clark, another bright and bubbly student, still friends with others from her year group. For a time I taught both her daughters when I returned on supply.

Caroline Jones(Knights) Her dad, Mick, was the former head of PE at Netherhall school, she also had a sister, Stephanie. Caroline was an amazing dancer, but I came across her again when she worked in a surveyor's office in Cambridge and helped with the purchase and sale of our house. So lovely to meet with Caroline, her daughter Chloe became a teacher and her son was also at the college, smashing kids just like their Mum.

Caroline Hunt Lindsell I met a few years ago in Burwell High street, I didn't recognise her but she remembered me from my time as her Year Tutor. She organised a very successful school reunion for her year group two years ago.

Kelly Rose is the only person I'm aware of who became a dentist
and yet when she was at the college I thought it was the arts and particularly drama that she excelled in. I was wrong. Kelly is a qualified dentist living in Cardiff. Would I let her fill one of my teeth? Absolutely I would, great girl and very conscientious.

Kim Ball posts some very interesting pictures on facebook, as she owns a houseboat. In my early days at the college, she took part in a prank with geography teacher Les Walke. He was one report missing from his form and it was from me, I told him I would send it over, asap, after a couple of obvious fake ones I sent Les the real missing report but not how he expected. My class carried over a large cardboard box that had been in the corridor in the Morris wing. When it arrived during his lesson the top opened and out jumped Kim holding the report! Classic, I hasten to add it was in my very early days and fortunately the hierarchy didn't get to hear about it. You couldn't make it up.

Ben Swann or Swanny as he is affectionately known. Very good friend to Chris and Shane, martial arts expert He worked with Chris at Babraham institute for a time. Shane and his mates like Andrew Lodziak, James Carter, and Rolfy (Jeremy) and other friends from their college days have occasional card games with Ben where money changes hands, not big stakes I don't think.

Lisa Rixon. Occasionally I would meet her walking to school in the morning. She lived in Teversham Way, a house which we bought after Lisa and her family moved on. I really liked the house which overlooked the green, Lisa now lives London.

Beverley Else (Thompson) lived just around the corner, Bev was so funny and she had a strong sense of justice. I recall one morning she caught up with me in Babraham road and complained all the way to school that a new video camera we had just purchased was always being used by the English department, I actually think it was there's anyway! Beverley was a member of my earlier drama group, she was great fun, and featured with her friend Andrea in a drama scene staged for the local press. I remember meeting Beverley in Ashley way a few years later holding her new born baby girl. Move on eleven years and Georgia came to the college and was in my history class. We looked at evidence one lesson and I showed them the picture of the staged photo twenty years previous. So then my class recreated the same photo in the same location with Georgia in her mum's place, Georgia now has children of her own and Bev Thompson is an active member of the Sawston community.

Pippa Bell pictured earlier in chorus, went on to be come a music teacher and Head of Year at a Cambridge school

Mark Judson, was never a pupil but an excellent art and pottery teacher, I know he loved teaching at Sawston Village College in the seventies, his favourite school and misses those days.

Kate Stephenson-Ellis accompanied Chris to the Leavers' Ball, her daughter Ava, was the first person to read my book *Saving Birdgirl*

Kayleigh Paske Retuned to the college as Lower school Secretary, having been a very valuable and supportive member of my year group, chocolate bars were our particular favourite with the morning coffee. It seemed strange the idea working alongside someone you used to teach but it worked brilliantly from day one, not just with me but with all the staff, a very confident and competent young lady. I used to teach Carol, Kayleigh's mum, she also has a brother Stuart. And many many cats!

Kayleigh Paske

Emma Frost who left us for the frozen wastes of Canada or somewhere near the North Pole. Daughter of Margaret Frost, former Deputy Head .
Emma has kept in contact and always writes amusing posts, I know she is a campaigner and animal lover.

Jackie Ifould (Kelly) who is a member of the Burwell reading group which I belong to, and I didn't realise that she was at the college for some time, They are a lovely group, we all meet once a month to discuss the chosen book and have a drink and get on very well.

Chapter Twenty Five

Falling Caterpillars and stars of the silver screen

So around 1984 I made my first film at Sawston Village College, using an 8mm movie camera. I bought the camera originally to record my family and my children growing up but decided to do a little filming at SVC. The films only lasted about 3 minutes and were silent, but they were in colour and so enough to give an impression of life and also a record. Trouble was each film had to be loaded into a projector, to be shown on a screen or white wall. It was fiddly and time consuming and it wasn't very practical. I filmed the buses coming in, the canteen and the history block. Some of students had put together a little scene in the classroom showing an argument over inter- form teams. The girl who thought up the idea and is shown in the centre of the group is Lindsay Brunnock as she was then, joined by Tanya Ward and Susie Nichols. Lindsay also inspired my first ever story. I knew she was a very talented girl but had no idea where this would lead to in the future, more about her in the chapter on TV and film.

We used an old slide projector in the history dept which was useful in lessons. Eventually, the English dept purchased its own video camera and there was another centrally based, which was fun to use from time to time. Again, the cameras were very large and the VHS tape snapped into a compartment at the side. After filming, you could show it straight away on a recorder attached to the television. Problem was always editing. Only feasible way to do this was to use two recorders connected by a cable and play the master through one recorder onto a blank tape in the second one. The quality of the picture often diminished on the copy tape but by using the counter, stopping and starting recording, you could make a reasonably final copy which could be shown in the classroom or hall. Reasonable that is by 1984 standards.

Soon afterwards as interest grew in video production in school, myself and Julie Warne,one of my colleagues did a video training course at Homerton on the techniques of filming and production. We then decided we would produce a drama. I wrote a script called Chain Reaction, a story about a school dance team competing in a local final. Julie helped direct the film and she also played a teacher. It was great fun, the two leads were played by Sally Whitaker and Francesca Owen as sisters, part of the home team known as Red Sky, and very good they were to. The lovely Judy Parnwell, lower school secretary and school nurse played their screen mum. Sadly Judy is no longer with us after passing away far too early. The back story was that the girls' dad had gone to prison and so there were a few confrontational scenes in the classroom as the day of the competition approached and the stress increased on the family. Sally played a typical, moody teenager always threatening to leave the team, Francesca, who was two years younger was her usual vibrant self, doing some wonderful back flips in the middle of her dance routine. Both girls gave fantastic performances. I was able to persuade Richard Craggs to play the teacher.

We filmed around Sawston, on the Icknield rec and in Princess Drive over a few afternoons when school ended but the main day was a full Saturday, filming the competition in the Lower School Hall. We used about forty extras who came long to cheer their team on. Music and props provided by Brendan and the two dancing groups were both from SVC. The home team comprising of Sally, Francesca, Cheryl Rush and Lucy Cavallo. The away team was captained by Kia Page, who since her dancing days has gone on to be come a rector in the Church of England in Surrey. Also in the away team was a young Vanessa Pesci, (Cross) Vanessa went on to form her own dance group and teaches in many local towns and villages, including GCSE dance at Sawston VC.

The groups did their own choreography which was superb. We did get VHS copies done of the tape and it turned out well overall and it was a good experience for both Julie and I and the cast. The credits were written in felt tip on a piece of cardboard with the song 'Chain Reaction' played over the top. It was the beginning.

Dr Mary Archer came to watch the film in the Walnut Room one morning and presented the trophy to Sally and Francesca. But it would be another three years before we produced our next film which was to be very different. But in the meantime I got a script filmed by BBC Schools Television. I was asked to write about friendship problems in the early secondary years, for a daytime programme called Tutorial Topics. The 20 minute film called Two's Company was shown twice on BBC2, and featured in the Radio times. In the cast as an extra was Melanie Blatt, I didn't know her at the time but she was later to become lead singer in the all girl group All Saints. It was filmed in a school in Notting Hill and also at the Jorvik Viking museum in York. I watched a day's filming in London. It was exciting seeing the BBC van outside, with a catering van. Sadly the series ended soon afterwards and I never had an opportunity to write more. Most of the writers for television were full time and or had an agent. Andrea Bade Clinton, a new pupil at the college who came from America helped me with the script as one of the cast was American.

Soon afterwards I became Head of Year and my writing was limited to one production a year. As a head of Year I had attended a conference on child abuse in Cambridge and found a lot of work needed to be done to educate staff and parents, and support the children who were suffering in some way. It was suggested I might write a film script based around child physical abuse, using actors from different schools. And it would be funded by the Henry Morris trust which supported young people through- out Cambridgeshire. I knew that this had to be a professional job. If I was going to do it I wanted to do it well. John Fussinger, who owned a local video company,Capri TV, offered to film the project for a very reasonable fee.

Anna Johnson, small and vulnerable, played the lead role of Stacey who runs away from home after being struck in the face by her mother, then stays out all night. Eventually she is placed in a refuge for teenagers whilst her case was being dealt with by social services. In this case we used the garden of a well known Sawston resident, Mary Challis, as a wildlife sanctuary. Today, Mary's house is now the Sawston museum. It was vital that I researched this properly and took the advice of trained professionals. And I knew we also had to widen our location search if we were to do justice to the story. I consulted with Sgt. David Robinson from Cambridge City Police and Yvonne Quirk, Advisory teacher from the Community Unit in Huntingdon. There was support too from Cambridgeshire County Council. What was paramount as the film was going to be shown in schools was that children could be reassured that in most cases they would not be taken away from their families and placed in a children's home permanently, and also the importance of telling someone if they were suffering abuse in anyway. We recruited Dan Strauss, a history teacher, to play the interviewing police officer. And the local police officer Ron MacDonald also played a part in the hunt for the run away child. Betty Cleveland worked on the make up. Anna looked beaten and bruised having stayed out all night, John did such a great job filming and editing the project, which we called *Wild Strawberries*

We filmed one evening after school which went on till about 8pm, we stopped for a break and I took Anna down to the fish shop in Sawston high street where we all got fish and chips, It was really funny because her face was heavily bruised thanks to Betty's brilliant and highly effective make up and I noticed other people were staring at us. I quickly explained this was for a film we were doing and I was not an abusive parent! I have to say it was a very emotional part and Anna was fantastic, taking it all in her stride. Her mum and Dad were also very supportive and gave their blessing to the project right from the start, I was and still am very proud of her. Later local television news came to interview us both at the college. And we did two radio interviews. Here she is filming:

However, we received a massive blow the week before filming begun when the Henry Morris trust withdrew funding at the last minute, it seemed that drama projects were not part of their remit, However, I was delighted when John Marven said the college would meet Capri's production costs and the money would be paid back through the sales of the video. Also, Mary Challis, bless her, sent us a £50 donation. And so the video went ahead We had a special showing at school covered by local press and radio and I was delighted with the result. I was grateful to all the people who supported us. But as this project ended John was already talking about filming a drama aimed at school children about the dangers of drug taking. He said if I wrote the script he would film it and edit it, and would waive his fee as he felt this was such an important topic. In 1995 we launched *Blue Twilight*, our most ambitious and controversial film to date.

The harrowing topic that John wanted to do was to tell of a teenage girl who dies after taking ecstasy at a party and we would film it during the summer holidays. We auditioned over forty girls for the lead role, and it went to Annabelle Roberts, a year ll student from the Perse school for Girls. I had seen Annabelle perform at the Cambridge drama festival and her Mum and Dad were well known members of a drama group in Whitlesford. Also joining the cast was Poppy Gaye, who played younger sister Cassie.

We filmed at Sawston VC and also one scene in our house in Teversham Way. We set up a party scene at a house in Trumpington which seemed funny creating a party at nine in the morning as the kids played very loud music and swigged alcohol from beer bottles (no alcohol was used). We used a cast of about a dozen. During the party Annabelle's character, Ashley, takes her first ecstasy pill. Soon afterwards she collapses. John did a great job with sound and strobe lighting, assisted by the wonderful Helen Barton. Cambridge Disco Hire provided the lights. After being sick, her friend calls an ambulance. We actually used cold vegetable soup which Annabelle had to drink. Yuk! We persuaded an ambulance crew to come and take her to Addenbrooke's hospital, I rode in the back, blue lights on, as John filmed Annabelle, her eyes barely open, and tubes down her throat. It was so realistic. For me I think the most moving moment came when one of the ambulance crew said 'Ashley, stay with us...She's gone unconscious.' I knew as the writer that Ashley wasn't coming back. The ambulance crew were fantastic but so may people felt it was such an important topic they were willing to give their time and services for free. But the best was yet to come in terms of support .

Addenbrooke's were willing to provide an emergency room and two doctors, providing there were no other emergencies at that time. They were ready and waiting, Dr Jane Robinson, head of A and E, and Dr Gregor Campbell Hewson with staff nurse Jacqueline Lynch. Annabelle was immediately transferred onto a table where they tried to resuscitate her, even using electric shocks. Sadly it failed and Ashley died on the operating table. Gosh it was hard for us to watch, even knowing it wasn't real, but such a harrowing part for Annabelle to play. And then we had to film mum telling telling a tearful Cassie that her sister had died. But John hadn't finished yet, to really hammer home his point he had arranged for a funeral car from Richard Stebbing's Funeral company to carry a coffin to Newmarket Road cemetery which we filmed from the main gate to a special plot, where John's local vicar was to conduct a short service. We had a few mourners playing extras standing by the graveside. It sounds very morbid but there were also humorous moments. The coffin was lowered into the ground with flowers thrown on the top and the vicar said

'we pray for our dearly departed brother Ashley may he receive the blessing... .' At which point we stopped filming and pointed out that Ashley was a girl! So the coffin bearers had to haul the coffin up again and we had to re- film that scene, much to our amusement, but for visitors watching the scene who had no idea what was going on it must have been very confusing!

John was so determined to get his message across that 'drugs kill' that he even dug a mock grave in his own garden in Histon, so he could film the final sequence from a camera hidden in a box representing a coffin in the ground that showed clods of earth being shovelled on top. It was quite something to see.

The film was very well received, with a lot of interest from the media. I was interviewed with members of the cast on both ITV Anglia News and BBC Look East. The highlight was a special showing of the film on a Saturday matinee at the Arts Cinema in Cambridge. Not everyone supported John's views, especially some educational advisers who criticised our heavy handed approach, and felt it was not suitable for young people and not the right way to educate them about the risk of drugs. But we believed we were producing something unique that had never been done before and as John said at the time, 'if it saves one life it's worth it. The film was used in PSHE at Sawston and many other local schools.

How ironic and very sad then, that just a few weeks after filming Blue Twilight, seventeen year old Essex schoolgirl Leah Betts died after taking an ecstasy tablet at a party. It was almost a carbon copy of our film drama.

I had to wait another seventeen years before making another film and this came from working with an outside independent film group.

Annabelle did a fantastic job and I worried that on occasions I was asking too much of her, but no she was very professional, always asked for advice and wasn't fazed by some of the shocking scenes she was asked to create. I loved working with Annabelle, a brilliant young actress, simply the best.
Annabelle recalls her dramatic role in her own words and what she has achieved since.

'I did a degree in Drama at Loughborough University and an MA in Performance at Mountview Academy. I have been a Supporting Artist/Extra in TV, film, and adverts. Mostly playing a member of the crowd and

shocked bystander but occasionally a small feature, frumpy maid and a 17th Century harlot being some of my favourites. I had a wonderful time touring TIE with a company called MOPA as we took Shakespeare to schools all over the country. I also tried my hand at small scale touring Panto, I still get flashbacks! Also, I acted in some fringe theatre productions in London and made some short films. In between I taught drama and ran music and play sessions. Most recently, I have returned to the stage, and I have been lucky to be involved with some amazing theatre companies in Cambridge.

When I was lucky enough to be offered the part of Ashley in Blue Twilight I was beyond excited. As a 16-year-old being given the opportunity to not only take on such a challenging role but also be involved in a project which could help raise awareness of the issues surrounding drug use was incredible. If ever I wanted to pursue a career in acting this sealed the deal. Being in front of the camera was an exciting place to be. We were all eager to learn and be part of something bigger than us. We were also very lucky to work with both John and Kelvin and absorb all the knowledge and direction we were given.

Filming the party and hospital scenes were challenging...acting being sick from taking the drugs many times on cold vegetable soup nearly made me go full method and throw up for real! I couldn't believe I got to ride in an ambulance and film in the Resus area of Addenbrookes. At the end of quite an intense filming day I returned home to find some sticky electrodes still stuck to me. This was long after I heard them call my time of death, waiting for "cut", my eyes closed lying on the bed being very, very still.

Witnessing the funeral was a surreal moment, standing behind the camera watching everyone stand around a grave, mourning. It was one that my mother found especially difficult; I can see why.

Along with the Arts Cinema film presentation (I still have the programme), various Q & A sessions we attended, and a news interview, it was and remains a very fond and vibrant memory. I hope it went some way in tackling the issues we were all troubled by. Mostly, a big thank you to Kelvin for taking a chance on casting me and continuing to create opportunities for young creatives to be involved in the arts.'

ANNABELLE ROBERTS

The pictures below come from location shots by cameraman John Fussinger

Scene from A and E at Addenbrooke's Operating theatre. Plus indoo party scene in Trumpington

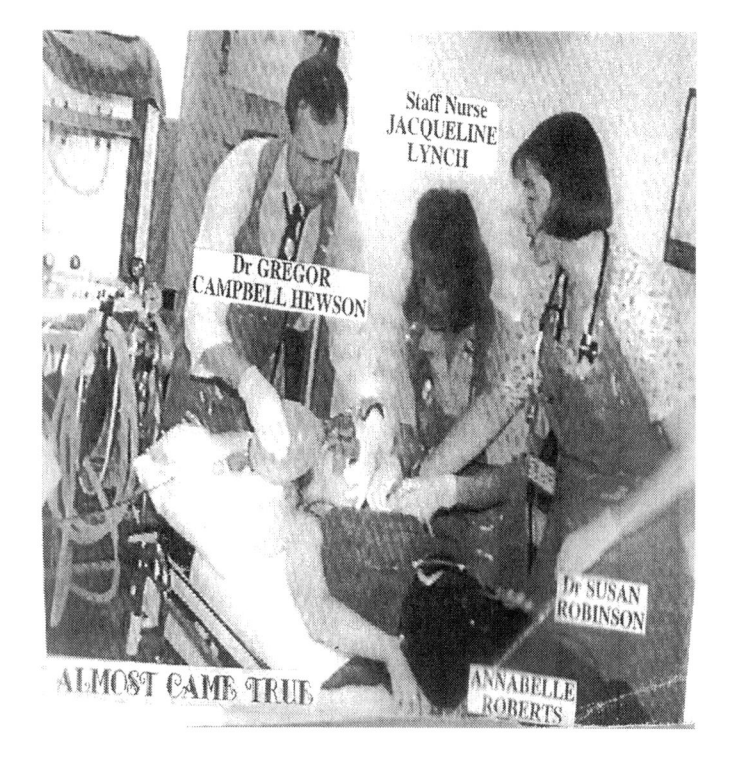

WE spent around two hours filming this scene, fantastic co-operation from the staff, so professional and supportive of our project. Poor Annabelle had to lie on the table playing dead all this time, Sadly, in current times there wouldn't be the opportunity to use the A and E today in this context.

Blue Twilight Support: Helena Johnson, Poppy Gaye, Jessica Fell

In the following scene Chris tries to help Annabelle as she becomes ill after taking ecstasy for the first time

Falling Caterpillars In 2011 although still on supply teaching at SVC although I had officially retired a year earlier, I joined a local Community Television group in Cambridge, who were aiming to produce a soap opera called *Cambridge Lives* for an independent channel. It was the idea of Fonz Chamberlain, who had auditioned and recruited a cast of over twenty people. I was given the part of a teacher, and later on when the script writer left the project I was asked to write the first script, which I did. However things didn't workout the way we hoped, Filming a drama is more difficult than a theatre production. The producers had to work with a number of different locations, all the casts were amateurs, and the sheer logistics getting everything and everyone in the right place caused problems and delays.

   Initially it was an excellent and ambitious idea but it was becoming clear that this was a project too far and after a few filming days, most of the material was not edited and apart from brief trailers no episode was completed or shown on screen. But it was enjoyable experience and I got the chance to share script writing with *Lauren Bishop,* a former student of mine, at Sawston.

Also with *Saffron Osborn-Clay,* who recently celebrated a wedding in the sunny Caribbean! She worked on the script, had a part and helped rehearse my scenes, it is a pity the production didn't work out.

But one good thing did emerge from *Cambridge Lives.* We decided to make a short independent film based on one of the scripts I had written about a girl who runs away and heads to Cambridge to trace her biological father who has ignored her all her life. We had already filmed some scenes earlier. And by luck, a wonderful cameraman David Johnson,who was part of our initial Cambridge Lives team, loved the idea . Our film was called *You Made Me*. I played the teacher dad, and my screen daughter was 15 year old **Olivia Reynolds,** relation, who I met on the Cambridge Lives set. Olivia was at Impington Village College and a member of Cambridge theatre group. A superb actress and a joy to work with. We filmed over four days, in the summer of 2011 using the Mill and the river down in Cambridge, also the George at Babraham and a special day out filming at Ramsey Raptor where Olivia's character, Coral, would be flying an eagle owl in the ring in front of a hundred spectators. It was a brilliant experience for us all. There was also one day's filming at Sawston VC, using a classroom and the play ground and field. Jazzie Lindsell, a fine actress, joined the cast along with David's daughter. My colleague, Adrian Lockwood, directed the scenes at Sawston including a fight scene between Olivia and Jazzie, which in my role I had to break up, and Coral swung a blow my way. Adrian decided that she would miss me, but somehow in the melee I wrenched my wrist. **Laura Bell** who featured in the film also directed sequences filmed in Cambridge.

David filming as Tilly(Jasmine Lindsell) confronts a drunken Coral, my screen daughter (Olivia Reynolds) No relation!

I was very grateful too for the support of Olivia's mum, Emma, who co-produced the film with me. David did a fantastic job on the edits and up loaded it YouTube, using a new company name Falling Caterpillar. The reason for the odd name is that when we were rehearsing shots for the film down by the Mill pond in Cambridge, Olivia sat under a beautiful weeping willow reading out the opening lines of Alice in Wonderland, when suddenly a large caterpillar fell from the tree and landed in her hair! From then on David decided to call the production after the Falling Caterpillar! We were very pleased with the final version which was shown at Sawston Cinema and later at the film club at the Maltings in Ely, afterwards Olivia and I were interviewed on BBC Radio. I was also very grateful that our Arts Manager Lesley Morgan at Sawston kindly lent us an expensive camera and tripod that belonged to the school. We borrowed the equipment for a week. What Lesley didn't know was on the first day of filming around the back streets behind King's Parade, I had removed the camera from the tripod for David to film close up walking scenes. When these shots were completed we adjourned for lunch and it was only when we were sitting down eating our sandwiches that I suddenly remembered I had left the tripod in the street. Having sprinted back I was so relieved to see it still standing on the pavement!

   I didn't get the opportunity to work with Olivia again who went on to sixth form before winning a place at Oxford University where she studied history of Art. However, Jazz was to feature in a lead role in our next film production called the Emma Rolfe story, based on true events from Victorian Cambridge. And once again David was to be the co- film director and editor. I researched and wrote the script about a young fifteen year old girl who lived in New street originally. She became a prostitute and often plied her trade along Newmarket Road using the pub on the corner, the Four Lamps. In 1876 Emma's story ended in tragedy when she met Robert Brownlng a former soldier from Mill Road who stabbed her to death, after meeting her on Midsummer common.

Filming with David Johnson and Issy Baker EMMA ROLFE STORY.

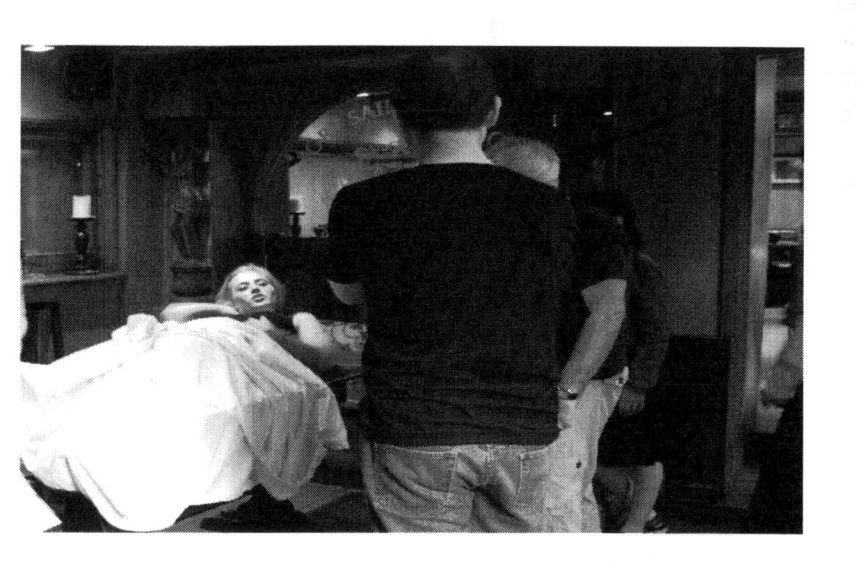

Filming inside The Fort St George where Emma's body was taken
Jasmine was a very patient corpse!

And below directing Max Reader in a scene with Gracie Freeman and Hattie Marshall

Max Reader, who was Jazz's boyfriend at the time who she had been dating since Year 10, played the part of Robert Browning. It was quite a dramatic scene. But they coped with it brilliantly. We were given permission by Greene King Brewers to film in the Fort St George public house on the common where Emma's body was taken after the murder and for the subsequent inquest. We filmed in the actual room used at the time. One actress, Frances Sayer, playing Emma's friend, did a lot of the make-up for the production, It was a challenge to actually film and produce an historical drama, especially such a violent one. But the supporting cast loved the film. Camilia O'Grady was the narrator and did a great job linking scenes from modern times back to 1876. We started filming at the graveside of Emma Rolfe who was buried in Mill Road cemetery, quite an eerie scene. You can still find her grave today.

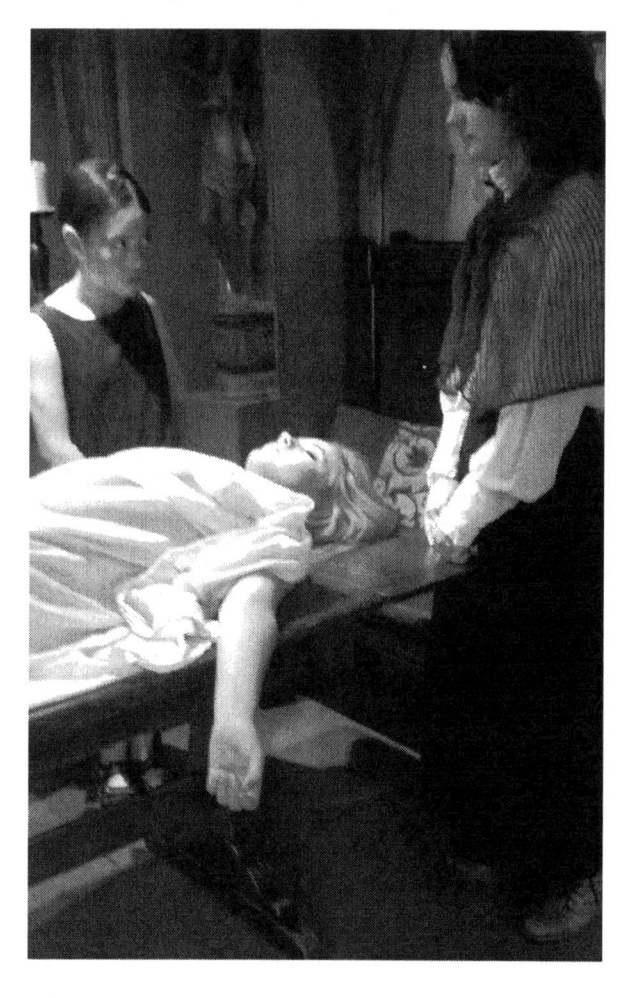

Young sister (Gaby Magee) and best friend (Frances Sayer) face the distressing scene witnessing Emma's body in the Fort St. George

Our base was at River Lane community hall, and we chose a quiet isolated area on nearby Stourbridge

Common for a lot of the Victorian scenes, which was ideal. But you can never avoid the sudden interruptions of an aircraft flying overhead or a police siren screaming close by. *CUT let's go again!* But it was great fun and despite losing one complete day of filming owing to a violent storm we completed in three days. It was also good to show the contrast between rich and the poor children and young adults at the time, Although I no longer had a group or a base at Sawston I was able to find additional cast from my former group at PQA Cambridge, Hattie Marshall, Gracie Chapman, and also my second cousins Phoebe and Maisie Runham Jones, whose mum, Naomi, did a fabulous job with costumes. And Gaby Magee played a nine year old thief, the sister of Emma. Also another cousin, Amba Reynolds, played a very well off young lady who wanted to do good and help the poor, while her boyfriend played by Vincent Lockwood was very cynical about the actions and lives of the lower classes. As a result I was interviewed at the Light cinema by a presenter from the newly formed Cambridge Television which showed the film on the local channel. in June 2014. Becca Baker helped with production and Tasha Cole was brilliant as one of Emma's friends.

David's company is now known as DMJ Imagery, and he has successfully filmed many new projects, both drama and documentary, since. I know we couldn't achieve what we did without David's pivotal role.
You can still view both You Made Me and the Emma Rolfe story on YouTube. Look for David's company or Falling Caterpillar production.

PQA stands for the Pauline Quirke Academy of Performing arts, currently situated in Parkside school in Cambridge, one of a number of venues nationwide. In 2013 the film and TV teacher had left unexpectedly at the beginning of term I was asked by a former SVC student Mark Tunstall who was a drama teacher at PQA, whether I might be interested in this role. I accepted straight away and met the Principal. I was very familiar with teaching and also directing and script writing but technology had moved on substantially since my earlier video days. Initially, I thought it would be for just a term but I stayed for 18 months teaching three different age groups every Saturday. I loved working for PQA ,and was fortunate enough to take part in a West End show at Her Majesty's theatre in London with other PQA groups, all contributing different segments of the show case, presided over by Pauline Quirke herself. Great experience for a young cast.

Next photo my second cousins Amba Reynolds, Phoebe Runham Jones, and Maisie Runham Jones, filming the Emma Rolfe Story

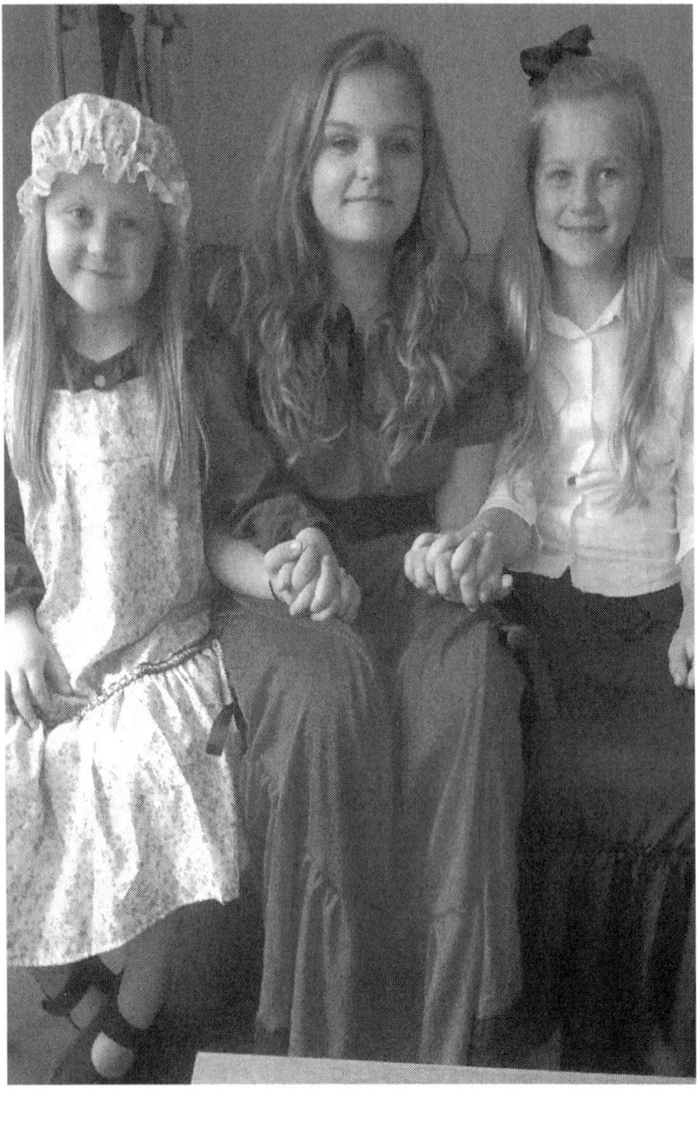

Chapter Twenty Six

From SVC to Film and TV.

Mark Tunstall. Mark studied at Middlesex University based at Trent Park as I did. He gained a major role in 2002 in the soap opera Brookside on Channel 4. Mark worked in many plays in various locations, he was also head of performing arts at Long road sixth form college. He was a drama teacher at PQA where I worked alongside him, I couldn't believe he still remembered his lines and the songs from the musical Last Flower on Earth from several years previous. Mark has currently just completed an independent film, great character lots of enthusiasm and talent.

Poppy Gaye. Poppy performed in school plays and shows. She was only 11 when she played the part of Cassie in our school video Blue Twilight, absolute delight to work with and a lively sense of humour. She played Griselda in the ITV hit series The *Worst Witch* and in an ITV drama *Coming Home,* Joanne Lumley played her mum and Keira Knightley her best friend in the production. Later Poppy went to live in the USA for a time, including working with the Rock. Her partner is film director Tom Hooper, who directed the *King's Speech.*

Poppy Gaye and Keira Knightley filming Coming Home for ITV

Steven Mackintosh very talented actor, left Sawston VC to take up a place at the famous Sylvia Young School in London, he played a part in *Adrian Mole's diary*. He has since been in many productions both for television and film. Sadly I never got to work with Steven as he moved schools before taking up the lead role in the pantomime, Jack in the Beanstalk, that Brian Higgins and I produced. I do recall one day when I was on duty in the Lower school office Steven appeared and said he had been sent out of English for day dreaming. Well, the dreams obviously worked!

Amy Rouse
Amy used to arrive at school early most mornings as she lived on a farm. She loved her sheep dogs and still does, took part in a BBC production One man or girl and her dog. Absolutely adores her animals, this was always going to be Amy's future. She runs her own dog grooming business now and is the owner of Candy's Candles. She is also a judge in sheepdog trials. But above all she has produced some fantastic pictures of her flock and her dogs. One girl's love for life.

Can't resist adding another of Amy's pictures!

Misty and Friends

Sean Lang Senior lecturer in History, author playwright, broadcaster from Cambridge 105 to mainstream American TV, if anyone needs a history expert Sean is the main man. It was a privilege to interview Sean on my Radio show at Addenbrooke's and we had tea and cakes afterwards. My nephew, Nick, said when he was studying A levels at Hills Road, it was Sean's inspirational teaching that led him to study the subject at University College London. Sean's daughter Emily was for a time Learning support assistant at at Sawston before moving on to study as a teacher.

Michael Barnard was in my year group 1996-2001,

very amusing and highly talented student in the arts, especially music. After studying drama he appeared in *Game of Thrones* as a torturer, a challenging part! He did his scenes so well that Sue had to go out of the room until it was over!

Chloe Pantazi-Wolber, performed in short plays at the college, and dance numbers, She went to New York and is currently working for Life magazine and she also does travel links and segments on American television, especially with a British angle. Chloe has done brilliantly, we still keep in contact. I visited her on work experience at a playgroup. By coincidence her mum was manager of the playgroup in Bourn where my grandsons went. Modest, hard working and very talented.

Jasmine Linsdell and Max Reader. They became an item in year 10, and got married very recently.. They did so much work in youth centre musicals and drama. Jasmine played a part in our film You Made Me, and took the lead in The Emma Rolfe story, set in Cambridge in 1876, shown on Cambridge Television. Max played Emma's murderer Robert Brownlie, fabulous performances from both. Jasmine and Max went on to study performing arts at East London. A class act!

Nick Saich so much enjoyed playing key roles in our stage productions, a born performer in my opinion in every way. Told he worked for the television shopping channel for a time. He currently does disco at the Shard every week, which I believe is a silent one.! Always reliable, always funny and Nick formed a great stage pertnership with Mark Tunstall.

Francesca Owen while still at Sawston VC, won a place at the Anna Scher theatre in London and I know she was highly rated by Anna. I recall her ringing me late one evening to tell me that she had just been offered a part to make a short film about the dangers of smoking available nationwide, directed by no less than David Bailey himself! She moved to Canada and has three children.

Katie Dermendjieva (Grimwade). Katie did go on to live the dream, working in theatre, on a cruise ship, and she also did a couple of TV and film adverts. She met her husband a juggler and acrobat at a circus performance. By coincidence, she moved into the next village where I live and is planning to run an after school drama group for key stage 1 and 2 in a local primary school. She was chosen as the poster girl for my first published play *The Teen Commandments.*

Matthew Hill shared our film night with a production that he wrote and directed. he did a lot of work for film club at Sawston with Lesley Morgan. He has since gone on to become a film maker himself and won awards at Sheffield University.

Anna Johnson was still at Shelford school when I first met her. Soon as I heard her perform I knew she was going to be special.

Anna played the lead in our video recorded by Capri TV called Wild Strawberries, which created a lot of local interest and was featured on Anglia News. (see Chapter entitled Falling Caterpillar)

Helena Johnson. Anna's sister, played the lead in our play *You Made Me,* and also briefly featured in the MAG segment on Channel 5. Helena went on to study at the Old Vic, and we wrote a play together called *High Spirits.* Anna continued to help and support the cast even if she didn't have a part. When *You Made Me* was published by Collins, Adrian and I dedicated the book to Anna and Helena Johnson. Their lovely mum and dad, Tony and Frances, took us out for a Chinese meal as a thank you for all the fun and experience the girls had had in our productions, such a lovely thing to do. After University, Anna became a teacher.

Katie Crawford. A teenage model,appeared in my play *Alys Incognito* and also featured in a story board with photos about bullying used in PSHE lessons. Recorded an advert in a magazine photo shoot on location in a train station. Went on to enter beauty contests and came third in Miss England, her photo with other candidates in the national press. Now with two daughters, Katie lives in the next village, her passion today is for horses.

Lauren Bishop, a former Sawston student, who graduated with a degree in film studies from Anglia University. Lauren is great fun to work with and brought many imaginative ideas to the plots She did a fabulous impersonation of Leona Lewis in the *Cambridge Lives* production. Lauren moved overseas to new pastures and we never had the chance to work together again. I think she's an influencer or a girl of mystery today!

Russell Ramsey joined our youth centre productions. He was given an excellent start at the college with his form tutors, including the support of his sister, Hayley. Russell went on to appear in TV and films, including a memorable scene with Ricky Gervais in *Extras*.

Frances Bowen Day. As a year 7 Fran played the part for the younger sister in *You Made Me*, As a result she was interviewed on the Channel 5 show with Sally Ann Kesiser She helped us so much, loved dance and drama, played Kia in Goodbye Blackberry Way, always good at sport, outstanding as a netball player. In sixth form she still came back to advise on movement and choreography, Fran left sixth form and gained a place at Jesus College Cambridge studying history. Lovely supportive parents Chris and Sue, we joined them for Fran's 18th birthday, then three years later celebrated her 21st breakfast party at Jesus College which was brilliant. Fantastic student and a real credit to the college. Sue and I took Fran and her friend Hayley Galvin to see Britney Spears perform at the London Arena, I could only get four tickets, fab night took forever to get out of the car park!

A few years later Fran's mum Sue did a sponsored walk across the Sahara for breast cancer and came into the college to talk to my geography class, later we put on a special show at SVC with Vanessa Cross' dance group followed by a Britney experience, performed by one of Vanessa's dance teachers

FRANCES BOWEN DAY

Camilia O'Grady My assistant at PQA was Camilia who featured in the Emma Rolfe story, great girl lots of imaginative ideas and brilliant with the kids Studied at Sawston VC and Parkside. We had a great time working together. Camilla used to cycle in all weathers from her home in Harston to Cambridge every week, but I always had some chocolate waiting for her and me at break time! Camilia is now living the dream, taking part in theatre productions and short films.

CAMILIA O'GRADY

Heather Craney Never had the chance to work with Heather but she worked on a few television productions including Vera Drake. Her older sister **Beverley** was a super member of my second year form, very reliable and I think went on to become a professional stage manager.

Suzie Curran in my opinion is the best act I ever seen on our pop idol show, her version of *New York* was just brilliant. After leaving the college, Suzie played a part in the Envision Community soap *Cambridge Lives,* which unfortunately didn't make it to the screen. Since then Suzie studied at Laine Theatre Arts school and now specialises as a choreographer and movement director for London performances and national theatre. Suzie is always smiling and I am so pleased that she is still so enthusiastic to pursue a life in show business. I've got a cup she gave me as a present with lots of stars on when she left the college, smashing girl. Of course I mustn't forget she has a very talented family, brother Tom, who helped with sound productions on our shows, studied at the Guildford School of Music. Tom was nominated at the Tony awards for best orchestrations for Six the musical in New York, And Johnny was a very good drummer, who played on stage at the college. As June Cannie said about them , 'A very talented family.'

SUZIE CURRAN

Tasha Malcolm-Brown Tasha organised a time capsule with year 7s for the millennium, a barrel which was sealed by Paul Morris in D and T and buried underneath concrete just outside the door to the Lower school office, I didn't record the exact spot and and I cannot find the photo of Tash and I with the capsule surrounded by others.

Tasha always wanted to be a writer in year 7 but at Uni she specialised in media presentation and did lots of film work. Later she joined Radio Cambridgeshire. When Kate and Prince William visited Cambridge I met Tash doing a live outside broadcast. Tash also did links for BBC Look East especially when she launched a project for the people of Nepal, a cause that is dear to her heart. When I was working at PQA Tash came along and did a workshop on television presentation with the group. Tash now works in the family firm, and is a local councillor in Pampisford I believe. I interviewed her on my radio show at Addenbrooke's, a smashing girl in every way, full of surprises and I'm sure we shall hear much more of Tash in the future.

TASHA MALCOLM-BROWN

Working for the BBC and taking over my Radio show!

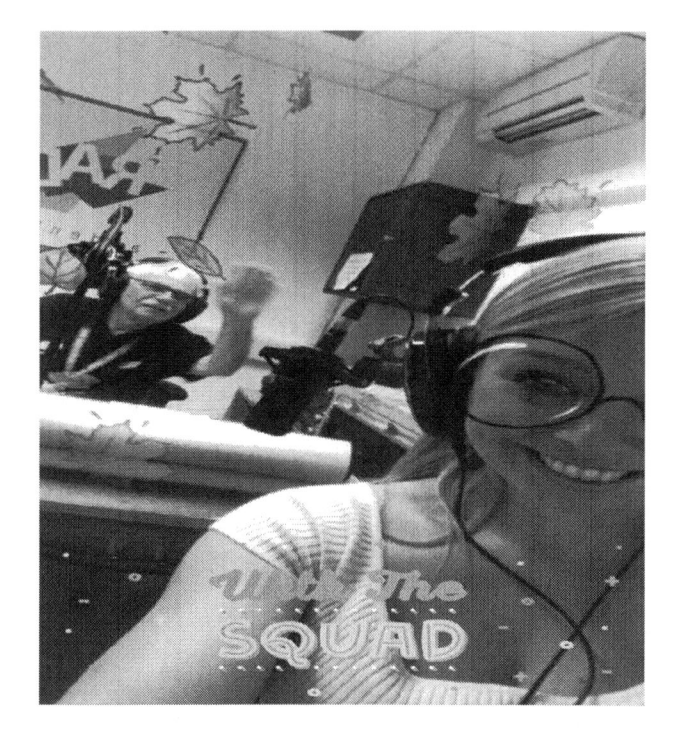

Tatyana Orrock Nunes Always a relaible and funny student, took part in many productions, my favourite being Face Value, playing Ruby. I used to see her sometimes in Sawston when she was walking up the by-pass to her student job at the local chicken joint, and where is she now? Living in the United States, Tatyana studied for a degree in History and Minor Criminal justice at University of North Texas. Fantastic achievement among other honours, I am very proud of her.

Lindsay Brunnock, is perhaps better known today as Lady Lindsay Branagh. She and Sir Kenneth married in 2003.

At school Lindsay was a very creative person and a good singer who appeared in lots of shows including Annie. She was also in my first silent movie and inspired my first story back in 1984.

She also did a brilliant assembly acting out the song

Eleanor Rigby highlighting loneliness in our society. In our first Talent show in 1974, one fabulous moment came when she did a duet with her friend Jackie Green, singing *Hey Big Spender,* they came down the stage and into the audience where Lindsay sat on Mr. Marven's lap, It was a surreal moment but the Warden took it all in good part, I think it brought the house down!

Lindsay worked as a designer and producer in television during the nineties before meeting her husband on the set of the film *Shackleton.* Lindsay stays out of the spotlight today, and is rarely seen in public. Once during a leap year, when Lindsay was about 13, she suddenly appeared with lots of her friends in front of me on the path outside the history block and going down on one knee, she held out a plastic ring and said :

'Mr Reynolds would you marry me?' The others shrieked with laughter. Lindsay was a great character, but don't tell Sir Kenneth about this incident! A great girl.

Chapter Twenty Seven

Being Andrea Bade (now Clinton)

I've been given permission to share Andrea's story below. When she first came to Sawston VC from the United State, around the age of 13, she was a very troubled girl who found it very difficult to fit in initially. Gradually she settled in and I was really pleased when she asked to join my drama group, working very well with others and contributing lots of ideas. In 1984 I was lucky enough to get a commission from BBC Schools Television to write a play about friendship problems for a series called Tutorial Topics broadcast on BB2. My play included a girl who arrives from USA, and I asked Andrea to assist with the script, to make sure I got the words right. She made a really useful contribution, was credited in the programme and photographed with me in the local news.

I lost contact with Andrea after she left school before we got together again on facebook by which time she had moved to America, I knew she was doing well in her life but I had no idea of the challenges ahead for her until I received this message not long ago.

Kelvin:

I just applied for a scholarship for my Masters degree. I wanted to share my personal essay with you - you remain the voice in my head:
Money, the necessary evil that creates and takes away opportunity. Today,

for me, that opportunity is an MBA. With $60,000 in student loans from my bachelor's degree as well as my daughters, considering a new loan is not feasible or practical. My company provides the opportunity to receive minimal financial assistance based on approval *of each course which is a valid potential. My husband says that we will "figure it out". And we will, we will figure it out because that is what I (and now we) do in the face of a challenge, we figure it out.*

What makes me a strong candidate for a scholarship? Nothing really, I do not consider myself more deserving than anyone else. However, I offer you a glimpse into what has shaped me and I hope that you will understand how providing assistance for this opportunity will be a worthy investment.

"You will never make it through High School", I heard when I rebelled at the world after my Mum died when I was 13.

"You will never have a career and be successful", I heard when I married at 18 and had a baby.

"You will never be happy and will regret this decision, I heard when I divorced and moved to the US when I was 23.

I did not hear the words "you will never graduate from college". The truth is no-one ever considered it to be a possibility, especially not me. College and higher education was for people that came from rich families with rock solid support systems and no responsibilities - I was just not good enough.

So, I worked and I provided and I started at the bottom. I progressed from receptionist to administrative assistant to project coordinator and somewhere along the way I thought "I am pretty good at this, I have found my talent". Applying for bigger roles was blocked by a lack of a college degree and I started to think, why not me? Community college and evening classes, juggling work, studying while being a single mom to a young child. I persevered - there were ups and downs it took me a long time but I made it through with my bachelor's degree. Me! A college degree! I could still hear the voices in my head of those that doubted I was capable of anything, much less making it through university. Many people have looked down on my education because it came from the University of Phoenix, but the work and experiences were no less and no matter what others said, I had the piece of paper that gave me opportunity.

I took that opportunity and became the best project manager I could be. I worked for companies large and small and gained and gave experience while continuing to grow as a leader. Today, years later, I lead a team of

Program Managers for a company that has one of the largest market values on the planet. I have created a global team who provides leadership for hugely impactful projects around the globe. Most importantly we stay humble and we find opportunities to teach our gift and raise up the next generation of leaders - no matter where their degree comes from. I have created for myself an opportunity that allows me to both lead and cultivate leadership and I am proud of what I have accomplished so far. It comes with new and different challenges that cause me to question if I measure up against my largely male colleagues. To the voices in my head, I say that growth is a journey and I am eager to learn.

In honor of Kelvin Reynolds my high school teacher and mentor who was a lone voice of support in my youth - today I can confidently say that I am good enough, I am deserving enough to be considered as a cohort for a Masters in Global Management at Arizona State University. I am confident that I have something to bring to the table that will impact those around me. I am confident that you will not regret investing in my future because I am will take this opportunity and create an impact on the world'.

I am so proud of Andrea and what she has achieved through her own determination and talent. She demonstrates how important it is to believe in yourself, and never give up. I am privileged that she mentions me in her application and that I have contributed something towards her journey. **Andrea, you are truly an inspiration for others.**

Kelvin's play gets a screening

Joan (left) and Jan toast their success.

SAWSTON teacher Kelvin Reynolds has had his first television script broadcast this week.

Mr Reynolds (36), who teaches English and history at Sawston Village College, sent a script for the popular children's series, "Grange Hill" to the BBC a year ago.

He was surprised and delighted when the BBC contacted him to write a script for a schools' programme, "Two's Company".

The 20-minute play was transmitted on Monday morning and is repeated today at 11.18 am.

The play is about friendship and jealousy. Sawston Village College pupil Andrea Bade (13), who was born in America, helped Mr Reynolds write lines for an American girl in the script.

Mr Reynolds, who lives in Princess Drive, Sawston, said: "I was delighted when I was asked to write the script, although it took a long time for the project to be completed. I first wrote the play last summer and it was filmed in London and York in October.

"It has been a great encouragement to keep persevering after a lot of rejections in three years of writing."

He is now working on a children's situation comedy and he said his pupils are an inspiration to him.

His drama group at the college has recorded a video of comedy sketches. The pupils, aged 11 to 14, including Andrea, wrote a lot of the material themselves, and it was directed by Mr Reynolds.

Sawston Village College teacher Kelvin Reynolds with pupils during a drama lesson. Mr Reynolds' play for schools' television is being broadcast by the BBC this morning.

Village news 2, 10 & 20 ● Kedington 4 ● Echo of the Past, Postbag 6 ● Linton 8 ● Stars 11 ● What's On 14 ● Clas

Next to me is Beverley Else (Thompson) and then Andrea

Chapter Twenty Eight

The Magic of Books

I wrote my first book for Amazon Kindle in 2012, called You Made Me, nothing to do with the play of the same name written by Adrian and myself. This story was based on a drama production a year earlier inspired by Olivia Reynolds, and set in Cambridge. The cover for the book originally featured Tasha Cole, a previous student, and the photo was taken by Becca Baker as part of her 'A' level project at Long Road. Three chapters of the book were written by Mia Dakin, a year 10 student at the time.

My personal favourite is *She's Not there*, a supernatural YA story that I started writing a few years back in 2002, and never got round to finishing it. This was published in 2017, and once again Becca provided a superb cover for the book, photographing a scared looking Stephanie Whittle. A picture of us on the photo shoot with the book cover below.

Since then I've added two more children's books, *Saving Birdgirl* and *Tyne's Victorian Adventure,* dedicated to **Molly Takacs**, who gave a lot of advice about circus acts and fire eating! Molly didn't come to the college but is a very inspiring and spiritual person, who I worked with on the *Cambridge Lives* Project. I am very privileged to call her a friend.

Saving Birdgirl is fiction but based on the character of the real Birdgirl, Mya-Rose Craig, who I had the privilege to meet last year at the Cambridge Literary Festival. Mya-Rose is currently studying at St. John's college in Cambridge.

And although she has now moved on to Linton VC, Jemima Price wrote a book when she was teaching at

Sawston called *Finding Ruby,* we have a copy at home.

In 2021 I wrote a one act play called *Controlling Marilyn Monroe,* for adults and young adults. I was very grateful to **Rikki Parry** who was in my year group who read the script and offered advice and shared our love for the legend that is Marilyn.

Published by Stageplays.com which can be downloaded online.

Chloe Miller, a London actress, model and dance teacher said she cried when she read my Marilyn script, I was very touched by that.

You can find my books on my Amazon page and thank you to everyone who has read them.

Chapter Twenty Nine

Tragedy

July 1983.

It's getting towards the end of term, my year 8 group are finishing their project on the plague and today they are copying out a Bill of Mortality from London in 1666 detailing the number of people who have died in the last week, and apart from the plague they list other causes of death. Sitting right at the front is Clare Goddard, a bright, imaginative and delightful little girl, who has also written and acted in comedy sketches for me for the school fête.

I'm feeling quite relaxed, humming a song by Leo Sayer *Orchard Road,*, Clare joins in and makes a humorous comment about my singing and the lyrics. She then tells me this will be her last lesson as she is going on holiday to the Scilly Isles the next day, she says the family go every year but this time it will be different as they will be flying in a helicopter from Penzance, just 20 minutes journey instead of taking the ferry.

'There's one problem though Mum really hates flying,' says Clare.

'Oh, she'll be fine, twenty minutes hardly any time at all. You'll have a lovely time,' I say.

At the end of the lesson I take her book in and wish her a lovely holiday.

I never saw her again.

On Sunday my neighbour, Hayley, told me that a helicopter had crashed just off the Scilly Isles and there were rumours that The Goddard family were on board. This was before the internet and mobile phones and I hadn't seen the news or any details. I played it down but somehow I knew.

I switched the radio on for the BBC lunchtime news,

'A helicopter has crashed into the sea a mile from its destination in the Scilly Isles. Out of twenty six people on board, twenty one people are known to have died in the crash, including the Goddard family from Saffron Walden with their children, Nicholas and Clare.'

My heart was broken
Only the youngest child in the family, Howard, survived the crash, losing both his parents and his brother and sister.

The final history lesson of term, I'm met by silence, many pupils are in tears. I look at the empty desk in front of me and say. 'I don't feel like teaching you today.' I take home Clare's exercise book and it's ages before I actually open it. Clare has copied out some of the entries from the Bill of Mortality which are listed in alphabetical order showing the causes of death in London that week. She has reached the letter D, her very last entry takes my breath away. It says *Drowned*

Many staff and friends from Sawston went to the funeral at Ickleton church where the family lived. It was unbearable.

Isn't it strange how sometimes small and insignificant things stay in your mind forever at a time of great trauma or tragedy? I still occasionally play the Leo Sayer song *Orchard Road* but for me it will always be Clare's song.

Over the years there have been other tragedies involving students from the college. Harley Winster from my year group died in 2001. His friends prepared a lovely page for him published in the year book,
And then there was Richard Ball who died in similar tragic circumstances.

I recall teaching a history group with just 21 students. They left in the summer term and within a few weeks, two of them, Nicola and Gary were killed in separate motorcycle accidents.

And very early on in my teaching career, Tracy Kerry, was killed aged only fourteen.

There have been others too, I can't imagine what it must be like for a parent to lose a child.

Helga Roberts

I have dedicated this book to the memory of Helga Roberts who was in my first form IR, and as I said at the beginning she was with me from Day one, my first day at Sawston Village College and Helga's.

Helga sat with her best friend Tanya Gale, both super girls, so helpful, friendly and very talented. They were like my class monitors in my first year. I was also involved in a drama production produced by the English department, called Out of the Crowd, and Helga and Tanya were dancers, I still have the programme.

Helga came to see me after she had recently left, she was thinking of a career in languages, possibly teaching. After gaining a place at Newnham College, Cambridge, Helga took a year's sabbatical to teach English in a Grammar school in Hamburg. One night in March 1986, after going out to a dance with her friends, Helga was walking the short distance back to her apartment when she was attacked and brutally murdered crossing a school playground. It was many years later before her attacker was found.

Helga had everything to live for. She was only 22 years old. Her tragic death stunned the local community in Hamburg. Hundreds of students and their teachers gathered by candle light to remember Helga in the main hall of the school with Helga's picture pinned to the blackboard at the front. Her father had the most awful job imaginable, he had to go to Germany and bring her home. Her funeral took place in the village of Ashdon, near Saffron Walden.

Always special, never forgotten.

Chapter Thirty

A Personal Journey

All three of our sons were educated at the Icknield School and Sawston Village College, where they made life long friends.

The photograph shows a year 7 trip to France in 1990. In the front row sits a boy with almost white hair, my eldest son, Shane. And moving one place to the right is Gillian Gallichan, resting her chin in her hands. Shane didn't know at the time nor did Gill that they were to marry sixteen years later! Although they weren't friends in Year 7 they were in the same form and I was their head of Year for one year. Later on, they were part of a group of ex-Sawston students who stayed friends but it wasn't until after University they got together and moved to Ickleton. Gill's mum, Pamela, worked in the office and reception at Stapleford school and her dad, Andrew, was a police sergeant. My first grandchild Sam, was born in 2007 and three years later Joel arrived.

NOW AND THEN!

Chris, my second son went to Uni at John Moores in Liverpool and in another coincidence he met the sister of Simon, who was in the same residential block as Chris. Gemma followed Chris to John Moores and they moved in together in Newton Le Willows, where they still live today. In 2014 Madeleine our granddaughter was the first girl born in my family for 52 years! So from then we travel regularly up the M6. Seb arrived in 2018.

David married Faye and they have Riley and Florence and live in Saffron Walden. Faye loves animals and after the children's hamster called Biscuit died recently Florence was heartbroken, they have a kitten now. So I called the gerbil in my earlier chapter Biscuit. David was in one of my drama productions and also an excellent footballer.

It's interesting that all my lovely daughter-in-laws have worked in schools, Gill as a TA although she is now a finance officer, Gemma is deputy head of a science department at a school in Merseyside and Faye is a TA in a secondary school and this year gained an A* in drama which she studied alongside the students in her class.

But not one of my sons became teachers, all choosing careers in computer programming, finance and insurance. I guess having a dad as a teacher in their school put them off for good! But its thanks to Sawston VC that Sue and I now have a large family and six grandchildren. Our personal legacy from SVC!

Paul and Kathy Hammond.

These two are our very special lifelong friends. Paul I mentioned in an earlier chapter. We met at the High school in 1963 where we became good friends. And it was Paul who got me the job at Ladd's café in Drummer street and also the little yellow caravan in the bus station. After Paul left, and moved to Hastings where he met his future wife Kathy, Sue came to work at the café. It it hadn't been for Paul getting me the Saturday job I probably would never have met Sue and our lives would have been very different.

Paul does have a connection with the college too. On Saturday mornings when I was manager of the Year 8 football team, Paul occasionally come over for home matches and run the line for me. (He was back in Cambridge then), And in my first year at Sawston, Paul, who worked in local government, came to deliver a lesson to my Year 11 Social and Economics group as part of their examination course, on how local finance is raised and managed in the community. It was the one and only time we have been teaching together!

And since those early days we have remained friends for sixty years.

Might have been my sixtieth and might have had a little too much Wine!

Chris, Gemma and family on the occasion of Madeleine's Communion.
Madeleine, in white in the centre, is the first girl born in my family for 52 years! Finley, the fabulous golden retriever is only one year old

Holiday at Home Farm in the Cotswolds, thanks to Pamela and Andrew. Youngest son David and Faye on right of the picture with granddaughter Florence, and to the left Sam, Riley and Joel, with Gill's family.

Flo having a wonderful time on her first riding lesson, I'm behind riding Izzy with my wonderful instructor, Debbie, making sure I'm on a tight rein literally! I'm getting better, I can trot now! Thank you Old Tiger Stables, Soham you are all brilliant.

John Marven

My first head or warden as he was known as, was John Marven. But no one ever called him John, all the staff referred to him as Mr Marven. He actually worked as an Education inspector originally at Shire Hall and I recall taking him a coffee on occasions, along with other senior staff when I was employed in local government. I don't think he remembered me though. Later when the previous Warden of the college resigned in the late sixties, the college was in a mess and its reputation was not good in the community. Mr Marven took over running the college for a couple of terms to stabilise the situation. A few months turned into 25 years! John turned the school around and established a brilliant reputation as one of the best schools in the county. I have so much to be grateful for to John Marven.

He gave me my first post, as a general subjects teacher, and a year later approved of my promotion to year tutor. In 1980 he made one of the staff houses available for Sue and I in Princess Drive, we left our rented house in Cambridge and moved to Sawston. which we eventually purchased from the housing association in 1984, staying in Sawston until 2012.

John taught a few lessons in physics and Maths, but never came into the classrooms. But he always knew what was going on and as Stan Webb, the Deputy Head, told us new recruits when we first arrived in 1975, 'There's only one boss here. Mr Marven.' I must also pay tribute to John's wife Janet, a lovely lady who taught French and came on several trips to France.

John was also very supportive of my drama and music shows, although when we did a school talent show which I co- produced I had no idea that Jackie Green and Lindsay Brunnock singing *Hey Big Spender* would come down off the stage and briefly sit on his knee. I was horrified at the time but it brought the house down and John saw the funny side.

I met him once or twice in town after he retired, and I was very pleased that he came to my retirement do that I shared with Sarah Konig. John died in 2018, his funeral service at St Mary's church, Sawston.

JOHN MARVEN

Meeting a new friend at Wandlebury

Conclusion

After a five year absence, I returned to Sawston VC in April this year to take a Year 11 assembly, the theme was Sawston in the seventies and how things have changed since my early days in teaching history. The students are studying this topic for their examination course. It was lovely being back at the invitation of the Head of History Sarah Jackson-Buckley, who I worked with previously on several occasions on supply. Always a lovely person to work alongside.

It did seem strange talking to a year group where I didn't recognise anyone and they didn't know me. But I felt it went well and the students were quite attentive. But what was also interesting is the response I got from former students from several years ago who commented on face book. One of whom sent me a lovely message I've included below.

So there you have it, 43 years teaching at the college, actually eight of which were on supply. As I said earlier, I can't remember every single incident or event, nor all the students from the thousands who made their way into my class room. I apologise if you feel you've been missed out in which case I am hoping to write a follow up in the spring including a memory board for students to share their observations, achievements, lifelong friendships and adventures from their school days. And sporting legends, This also applies to the staff as I've focused in this book on the most important people in any school-the students. I know that I am very lucky to have worked at Sawston Village College for over four decades! It has defined my life.

It's been a fantastic journey for me over the years and I am grateful for all the former students who have kept in touch on social media, mainly facebook and sent me some lovely messages. And as I have tried to reflect in the book, I always love hearing of peoples' success and achievements since leaving the college. School is not always the best years of your life. It isn't for everyone. As Derek Cupit once told me 'You can't win them all but you can have a darn good try.' I certainly had my stressful days and a couple of times felt like walking away from teaching. Fortunately, it was only a temporary thought!

I was lucky to work alongside some amazing staff, and I know that teachers are doing a fantastic job today, the pressure mounts every year plus the fact that schools have gone through a very difficult time during the pandemic, which is still having major repercussions in many areas of education.

And so finally I would like to share this message on my timeline in April from **Clare Driver**

'I could only wish to be eleven years old again with you as my teacher. You were always our inspiration and we loved and respected you, I hope we showed you. I have a life long love of history as a result of your enthusiasm and great support, being my champion to push for me to do O level and a kind ear and word when my mum and dad's marriage collapsed and I needed a bit of guidance.

I have such happy memories of SVC as well as my lifelong friends and you're a big part of that x.'

Amazing message which means the world to me.

Thank you so much Clare

If I was starting now as a teacher I'm certain I couldn't last 43 years! It is a difficult job, very hard work and yes, at times very stressful. But I wouldn't change a thing. When I walked into the classroom and closed the door I knew I was doing the best job in the world.

Thank you Everyone

Kelvin Reynolds   2023

ACKNOWLEDGEMENTS:

I would like to thank the following for their help in producing this book.
Jacqueline Mordue from the Cambridgeshire Collection, The Cambridge News. The Haverhill Echo, Sawston Reporter.
BBC Look East and ITV Anglia News, John Fussinger Capri TV-Video, David Johnson, DMG Imagery.
Cambridge Television, Channel 5 The Mag
Mary Challis and the Challis garden Sawston.
The Stage and Television Today,The Times Newspaper and the Daily Mail.
Oxford University Press, HarperCollins Eduction and Letts publications. Carolyn Plant
Becca Baker and Helen Barton. Journalist Susan Elkin. Paul Morris. Sally Ann Kaiser. The Fort St George, Cambridge. The Arts Cinema, Cambridge.

And. of course, the people of Sawston who made it all possible.

222

Printed in Great Britain
by Amazon